Easy Real-Food Bento Lunches
for Kids on the Go

The
Little
Lunchbox
Cookbook

Renee Kohley

Author of *Nourished Beginnings Baby Food* and
Founder of Raising Generation Nourished

PAGE STREET
PUBLISHING CO.

PAGE STREET
PUBLISHING CO.

Dedication

To my husband and three little ladies, who took on this family writing project together as a team. You are my favorite taste testers, kitchen cleanup crew, and goal setters on this planet.

Contents

Introduction

It all started during my eleven-year-old's first year of school. Kindergarten. I remember being pretty geeked about packing lunches, and the first week or two it was so exciting. Being a child of the '80s and spending my teens in the '90s, I discovered that this lunchbox thing had gotten pretty cool since I had finished school. I would even go as far as to say it had become beautiful and fun, instead of the wrinkled-up brown paper bags (that squished each and every lunch item) that we all grew up with.

It was about two full months into my daughter's kindergarten year before it hit me. You know what I'm talking about: blankly staring into the lunchbox and wondering, "What in the world am I supposed to put in here? I have to pack this thing again?" Because as beautiful as that lunchbox was, I still needed to fill those compartments. And the parents of today are doing that whole "know better, do better" thing—we know our kids need more than a bag of chips and an apple to get through the school day.

But I still had an infant and a preschooler at home (who apparently needed lunch too!), and I couldn't spend all day preparing my kindergartener's lunchbox. I started creating a rhythm and a rotation to our lunch routine that was both exciting with variety and nutrients and predictable so that I could still live in the unpredictability that is a household filled with little people.

There was also the time struggle. I learned really fast that the quickest way to lunchbox burnout was making every single thing from scratch. While I wanted to include real, whole foods, it just wasn't realistic to scratch-make everything. It was like I was trapped somewhere between throwing Twinkies® in a brown paper sack and creating elaborate "Pinterest Mom" bento box works of art.

There is a better way, dear momma. There is a happy medium. You absolutely can pack school lunches that nourish your growing children and can be packed on a busy schedule.

My biggest goal for each lunchbox represented in this book (besides being filled with a balanced, whole-food meal that kids will eat!) was for each lunchbox to have just one homemade item. I want this book to be actually used. By real moms and dads. In the real world. With real schedules. One homemade item per box is realistic! So each box will show you how to make the homemade item, many of which can be made in advance or in big batches, and then how to balance the box with side items to fill in the rest of your child's nutrient needs. There is plenty of wiggle room within each lunchbox to make it your own too.

So what is a balanced lunchbox, anyway? My answer to you would be this: Don't complicate it.

Healthy fats, proteins, and carbohydrates—they all matter when it comes to kids, and in this cookbook, you will see a simple balance of these macronutrients. It's all about the ratio that works for your kids. This will look different for each family, and possibly for each child within your family. We are talking about children without inflammatory diseases or other health considerations. There are special circumstances where a special diet benefits a child.

But for most children, a good balance of all three macros is the key to stable moods and blood sugars, really good sleep, and laser focus for every life activity.

Keep in mind that growth spurts or seasons of stress and extra physical activity will make the macro ratio vary for your child. Listen to their body. Kids are smart—most of them don't live to eat, they eat to live. And they crave what their body needs at that very moment. The serving sizes of the food you pack may look different than what is represented in the photos in this book. In fact, your own children will ebb and flow from week to week or month to month depending on growth spurts and nutrient needs.

A simple way to approach lunch-packing would be the motto, "Make every bite count!" When you look at that lunchbox, are all three macros represented in a healthy way? If so, you are on your way, and it truly is that simple.

You will find that the food philosophy in this cookbook revolves around simple, real food within the three macronutrients. Fresh vegetables and fruit purchased in season, depending on where you live, will allow you to stay within your budget while keeping a variety of nutrients in your children's meals. Finding a good source for pastured meat, eggs, and dairy will ensure that the quality of nourishing fat and quantity of vitamins and minerals is top-notch. I have found that asking around at farmers' markets or using the Eatwild (eatwild.com) or Real Milk (realmilk.com) websites are helpful in finding these sources. While properly sourced wheat is not bad, all of the recipes in this book are gluten-free to ensure that children in schools that have to be safe for kids with celiac disease can still make the recipes and safely bring them to school. If you tolerate gluten, you can play around with the baking recipes and try wheat flour (preferably einkorn wheat). The recipes in this cookbook are also nut-free and school safe. Though nuts are not inherently bad for some, nut allergies are so common these days that many schools do not allow them. I wanted each and every recipe to be safe for these children. If your school does not have a nut-free rule, feel free to add nuts to the recipes! And because I know so many families that I come in contact with on a daily basis do not do well with dairy, the majority of the recipes in this cookbook are dairy-free or have a dairy-free swap. If you tolerate dairy, a well-sourced grass-fed dairy swap is perfectly fine.

Getting started packing real-food lunchboxes is as easy as deciding to take one baby step at a time. I have found that making one small change instead of a whirlwind overhaul is key to success. Planning and packing lunches can be done without overwhelming time in the kitchen. I promise. I don't have time for it, and kitchen work is part of my job!

Here are a few tips to rely on as you get started on this lunchbox adventure:

- Don't change everything overnight. Even if you are a jump-in-with-both-feet kind of person. Start out swapping one or two of your child's favorites (such as swapping frozen pizza for my Fun Friday Pizza Paninis [page 30] or using the Lunchables® Copycat recipes instead of the store-bought boxes) and trying one new thing in the lunchbox at a time. Changing the entire way they eat in one shot is sure to end in a fight.

- Try new foods at home first. The home environment is always going to be more comfortable than school. Instead of throwing kids a curveball with brand-new food they've never seen before at school, make it and eat it together at home first. You'll be surprised at what you make for dinner and they ask for in their lunchbox for leftovers!

- Sit down with the whole family and make a menu together. Everyone gets a favorite somewhere in the week. This is a family cookbook—it is for each and every person in the household. Curl up on the couch or circle around the kitchen table and have a family meeting. Talk to your kids about your "why." Why does lunch matter, and why does creating a family menu matter? Teach them about their growing bodies. They are never too young to learn, and they will blow you away with how much they are capable of understanding. Tell them that you care about how their bodies feel, and that you want to help them figure out what foods help them focus the best when they are at school. We have all felt a sugar crash or low energy—put that into words for them and help them become aware of the connection between their fuel and how their bodies feel. And then ask your kids their "why." Ask them about what they do all day at school and at extracurriculars, and help them see the correlation between when their body is fueled well and when it is not. Then create a menu. Together. Not as a free-for-all, but as a team. You're the chef and they are the sous chefs. Give them two or three specific options to choose from, such as, "We can have potato soup or alphabet soup for dinner this week that will get packed into thermoses for lunch on Thursday. Which would you like?" Let them help you write up the menu on a calendar.

- Don't shy away from a rotation. Once you figure out your rhythm, it is like autopilot and it is so nice—trust me! You can still get lots of variety within the same theme by switching in-season veggies and fruit and so on. A rotation can be as simple as having "Sandwich Surprise Tuesday" and "Thermos Thursday." The kids can help you fill in what sandwich and soup they want. Side items can be filled in based on what is in season or what you have in the house; you have a framework so that you aren't going into each week blind. Don't overthink it!

You can make every bite count with nutrient-dense, whole foods that have fun, kid-friendly presentations and flavors. You can feed the whole family nourishing food that helps their bodies grow without spending all day in the kitchen. Your kids will light up when they open their lunchboxes, and they will be ready to tackle their afternoon full and focused because of simple, whole foods that nourish their brains.

My vision is for the pages of this book to be dog-eared, dripped on, written on, faded, and loved on so much that this cookbook becomes a permanent fixture on your counter. I want your kids to be able to point to their favorite recipe. I want your menu plan to become a rhythm of recipe rotations from the pages of this book. I want this cookbook to be a framework to become your family's cookbook by making swaps and additions according to your family's tastes. You are the reason this generation is going to know how to fuel their bodies to feel well. It starts with you. You will be rewarded with children that are nourished to grow and know what foods make them feel their best.

Renee Kohley

Beyond Peanut Butter and Jelly
Fun and Delicious Sandwiches

Here's where the lunchbox rut ends!

I've been there, dear momma. Life gets busy, your brain is overloaded, and that good ol' peanut butter and jelly is such a reliable standby. There is absolutely nothing wrong with a little PB&J throughout the week, but bringing some nourishing variety into your routine is easier than you think. This list of easy-to-prep, nourishing sandwiches is my gift to you to put your sandwich packing on autopilot. Make a rotation that the kids love, and even on your most jam-packed day you won't have to think about what's for lunch.

From fun-to-eat chicken salad pinwheels (page 12) and club sandwich skewers with eye-appealing and easy-to-prep presentations (page 26), to Fun Friday Pizza Paninis (page 30), to Garden Party Quesadillas (page 20), to a McDonald's™ breakfast sandwich look-alike (page 19), you'll keep your sandwich routine fresh with new ideas — and more importantly, your kids' lunchboxes will be loaded with nutrient-dense food to fuel growing brains that have worked hard in school all morning.

How to Pack These Delicious Sandwiches for a Balanced Lunchbox

With the exception of the Garden Party Quesadillas (page 20), all of the sandwich concepts in this section are a good source of protein and fat. Simply add some side veggies and fruit of your choice, and you've got a balanced lunchbox for growing kids. Veggie sticks with dip and in-season fruit are easy, nutritious options. In the case of the quesadillas, adding a handful of mixed nuts and/or seeds, Fast-Prep Healthy Trail Mix (page 125), or some leftover chicken from dinner will bump up the protein. Or put a condiment container with nut butter or seed butter with apple slices for dipping.

Healthy Chicken Salad Pinwheels

(dairy-free, gluten-free, nut-free option, soy-free)

This fun and easy pinwheel presentation with fun colors and delicious flavor will make your little ones smile! Packed with protein and easy to eat, the kids will be ready to take on the rest of their school afternoon full and focused.

3 cups (420 g) coarsely cubed cooked chicken (see Notes)

½ cup (110 g) mayonnaise of choice (such as Easy Homemade Mayo Two Ways [page 159] or store-bought avocado or olive oil mayo like Sir Kensington's or Primal Kitchen brands)

1 to 2 green onions, coarsely chopped

½ cup (60 g) pecans (see Notes)

½ cup (50 g) purple grapes (see Notes)

½ tsp sea salt, or as needed

Black pepper, as needed

4 gluten-free tortilla wraps of choice (such as Food for Life brand brown rice tortillas or Sami's Bakery Millet and Flax Lavash)

In a food processor or blender, combine the chicken, mayonnaise, green onions, pecans, grapes, sea salt, and black pepper. Pulse 5 to 7 times to combine the ingredients. You don't want big chunks; the mixture needs to be spreadable. You can process the ingredients until they are completely smooth, or you can leave a chunkier texture for visual appeal.

Spread a thin layer of the chicken salad on a tortilla wrap and, starting at one end, tightly roll the tortilla wrap all the way up. (If your tortilla wrap does not roll well without cracking, moisten it slightly and heat it up a bit in a warm skillet or in the microwave for 10 seconds to soften it.) Set the wrapped tortilla on a plate and continue this process with the rest of the chicken salad and tortilla wraps.

Tightly cover the plate of chicken wraps with plastic wrap (or put the wraps in an airtight container), and transfer the plate to the refrigerator to chill and firm up for at least 30 minutes. You can do this the night before or 1 to 2 days in advance.

After the wraps have chilled, use a serrated knife to cut the wraps into 1- to 2-inch (2.5- to 5-cm)-long pinwheels.

Notes

- You can use leftover chicken from dinner using the Prep-Day Whole Chicken Two Ways recipe (page 164).

- For the nut-free option, use raw unsalted sunflower seeds or raw pumpkin seeds, or simply leave that ingredient out.

- Apples work well in place of the grapes.

Colorful Rainbow Pinwheels

(dairy-free option, gluten-free, nut-free, soy-free)

Brighten up your kids' lunchboxes and put a smile on their faces with these veggie-packed pinwheels! Colorful, mineral-rich veggies are speckled throughout the ranch-flavored spread that is packed with sustaining protein and brain-boosting healthy fat.

Makes approximately 20 pinwheels (depending on the size of the tortillas)

1 cup (165 g) canned or home-cooked chickpeas (page 163), drained and rinsed if needed

8 oz (227 g) full-fat cream cheese at room temperature (see Notes)

1 heaping cup (175 g) diced or shredded vegetables (such as shredded carrots, finely chopped broccoli florets, shredded purple cabbage, diced red and yellow bell peppers)

1 tsp onion powder

1 tsp dried parsley

½ tsp garlic powder

½ tsp sea salt, or as needed

Pinch of black pepper, or as needed

4 to 5 gluten-free tortilla wraps of choice (such as Food for Life brand brown rice tortillas or Sami's Bakery Millet and Flax Lavash)

In a small bowl, use the back of a fork to smash the chickpeas smooth. (Alternatively, you can use a food processor or blender to blend the chickpeas.) Add the cream cheese, vegetables, onion powder, parsley, garlic powder, sea salt, and black pepper to the chickpeas. Mix until the ingredients are well combined.

Spread about ¼ cup (60 g) of the cream cheese mixture on a tortilla wrap in an even layer and, starting at one end, tightly roll the wrap all the way up. (If your tortilla wrap does not roll well without cracking, moisten it slightly and heat it up a bit in a warm skillet or in the microwave for 10 seconds to soften it.) Set the wrapped tortilla on a plate and continue this process with the rest of the cream cheese mixture and tortilla wraps.

Tightly cover the plate of wraps with plastic wrap (or put the wraps in an airtight container), and transfer the plate to the refrigerator to chill and firm up for at least 30 minutes. You can do this the night before or 1 to 2 days in advance.

After the wraps have chilled, use a serrated knife to cut the wraps into 1- to 2-inch (2.5- to 5-cm)-long pinwheels. Store leftover pinwheels in an airtight container in the refrigerator for 5 days.

Notes

- To make the pinwheels dairy-free, use an all-bean spread like hummus. Some people that are dairy-free tolerate goat's milk, so a spreadable goat cheese would be an option for them.
- White beans would work in place of the chickpeas if they are what you have.

Kid-Approved Apple and Tuna Salad Wraps

(dairy-free, gluten-free, nut-free option, soy-free)

Brain-boosting power is on the way with this fun and flavorful tuna salad wrap, loaded with omega-3 fatty acids for nourishing growing nervous systems. With fun bites of sweet apples and crispy pecans, the kids will enjoy every mouthful of this nutrient-dense tuna wrap!

**Makes 5 (½-cup [78-g]) servings of tuna salad
(smaller children will eat about ¼ cup [39 g] per serving)**

2 (5-oz [142-g]) cans wild-caught tuna packed in water, drained

1 small apple, unpeeled, cored, and diced

⅓ cup (40 g) pecans, crushed (see Notes)

⅓ cup (73 g) mayonnaise of choice (such as Easy Homemade Mayo Two Ways [page 159] or store-bought avocado or olive oil mayo like Sir Kensington's or Primal Kitchen brands)

2 to 3 tsp (10 to 15 g) yellow mustard

¼ tsp onion powder

Pinch of sea salt, or as needed

Lettuce, as needed

4 to 5 gluten-free tortilla wraps of choice (such as Food for Life brand brown rice tortillas or Sami's Bakery Millet and Flax Lavash)

Cheese, tomato, or other toppings, as needed (optional)

In a small bowl, use a fork to break up the tuna. Add the apple, pecans, mayonnaise, mustard, onion powder, and sea salt and stir to combine. Taste the tuna salad and add more sea salt if needed.

To make the wraps, place the lettuce on a tortilla wrap. Add the tuna salad and the cheese, tomato, or any other toppings (if using) before rolling up the tortilla wrap tightly. (If your tortilla wrap does not roll well without cracking, moisten it slightly and heat it up a bit in a warm skillet or in the microwave for 10 seconds to soften it.) The tuna salad lasts 3 days in the refrigerator when stored in an airtight container.

Notes

- For the nut-free option, use raw unsalted sunflower seeds or raw pumpkin seeds, or simply leave that ingredient out.
- You can blend the tuna salad smooth to spread it on the wrap if your kids prefer that texture to the chunkier version.
- Tuna salad also works great on your favorite sandwich bread or just packed into a leakproof container with crackers to scoop!

Buttermilk Biscuit Breakfast-for-Lunch Sammy

(dairy-free option, egg-free option, gluten-free, nut-free, soy-free)

Drive-through fast food has nothing on these delicious breakfast sandwiches—both in nutrition and taste! The biscuits are soft with a great chew, and they hold up well after being frozen and thawed. Pile them high with the kids' breakfast favorites.

Makes 10 (2½-inch [6-cm]-diameter) biscuits

Biscuits

2 cups (244 g) Namaste Perfect Flour Blend, plus more as needed

1 tbsp (12 g) aluminum-free baking powder

1 tsp sea salt

2 tsp (10 ml) raw honey

1½ cups (360 ml) buttermilk or 1¼ cups (300 ml) cream or coconut milk combined with 2 tbsp (30 ml) apple cider vinegar, plus 1 tbsp (15 ml) buttermilk, cream, or coconut milk, divided

Breakfast Sammy

Scrambled egg rounds, as needed (optional)

Cooked sausage rounds or bacon strips, as needed

Cheese of choice, as needed (optional)

Preheat the oven to 450°F (232°C), and line a baking sheet with Silpat or unbleached parchment paper.

To make the biscuits, place the flour in a medium bowl (I recommend using only Namaste brand flour, since different blends will have different results in this recipe). Add the baking powder, sea salt, honey, and 1½ cups (360 ml) of the buttermilk to the bowl and use a rubber spatula to combine the ingredients until it just comes together into a sticky dough—be careful not to overmix.

Lay a silicone baking mat or a piece of parchment paper on a work surface and dust it with additional flour. Flour your hands and put about ¼ cup (60 g) of the dough on the floured surface. Place another ¼ cup (60 g) of dough on top and gently pat it down. Continue layering ¼-cup (60-g) pieces of dough, using the palms of your hands to form the layers into a round shape, until you end up with a round of dough that is at least 1 inch (2.5 cm) high.

Use a floured 2½- to 3-inch (6- to 7.5-cm) round biscuit cutter to sharply cut into the dough to make biscuits. Lay them on the prepared baking sheet. You'll have dough left over to layer again to make more biscuits until you run out of dough. Brush the tops of the biscuits with the remaining 1 tablespoon (15 ml) of buttermilk.

Bake the biscuits for 14 to 15 minutes for small biscuits and 16 to 17 minutes for large biscuits, until they are a light golden brown.

To make the breakfast sammy, slice a biscuit in half and layer the scrambled egg rounds (if using), sausage rounds, and cheese (if using), then top the sammy with the other half of the biscuit.

To freeze the biscuits, cool them completely, slice them in half, and store them in a freezer-safe bag for up to 3 months. You can then make a sammy with the frozen sliced biscuits, which will thaw by lunchtime no problem.

Garden Party Quesadillas

(egg-free, gluten-free, nut-free, soy-free)

Even the toughest little people veggie critics in the house will fall in love with these ooey-gooey quesadillas! There is something magical that happens to veggies when you roast them, as they become sweet with the caramelized sugars that naturally occur in the vegetables. Soft, easy-to-eat roasted vegetables, yummy cheese, and a creamy protein-packed bean spread make these quesadillas a well-rounded (and fun) lunchbox idea for any day of the week.

Makes 4 to 6 quesadillas (depending on the size of the tortillas; older children will eat 1 or 2 tortillas while younger children will eat ½ of a tortilla)

Roasted Vegetables

2 medium bell peppers (any color), cut into thin strips

2 small sweet potatoes, peeled or unpeeled and cut into ¼-inch (6-mm)-thick rounds

¼ small head cabbage, cut into thin strips

2 tbsp (30 ml) olive oil

2 tsp (6 g) taco seasoning

1 tsp onion powder

1 tsp garlic powder

Sea salt, as needed

Black pepper, as needed

Black Bean Spread

1½ cups (90 g) canned or home-cooked black beans (page 163), drained and rinsed if needed

2 tbsp (30 g) softened full-fat cream cheese or sour cream

1 tbsp (15 ml) fresh lime juice

½ tsp sea salt

¼ to ½ tsp garlic powder

To make the roasted vegetables, preheat the oven to 425°F (218°C). On a large baking sheet, toss the bell peppers, sweet potatoes, and cabbage with the oil, taco seasoning, onion powder, garlic powder, sea salt, and black pepper. Roast the vegetables for 20 minutes, until they are soft and slightly caramelized.

While the veggies are roasting, make the black bean spread. Combine the black beans, cream cheese, lime juice, sea salt, and garlic powder in a shallow bowl and smash the ingredients with the back of a fork until the ingredients are incorporated well and the mixture is smooth enough to spread. Taste the spread and adjust the seasonings as needed.

(continued)

Quesadillas

2 to 3 tbsp (30 to 45 ml) melted ghee, melted butter, olive oil, or coconut oil

4 to 6 tortillas of choice (such as Food for Life brand brown rice tortillas or Sami's Bakery Millet and Flax Lavash)

1½ cups (180 g) shredded cheese of choice

Full-fat sour cream, as needed (optional)

Guacamole (page 37), as needed (optional)

Salsa, as needed (optional)

To assemble the quesadillas, heat the ghee in a medium skillet over medium-high heat. While the skillet is heating, spread the black bean spread over half of a tortilla. Top the black bean spread with the roasted vegetables. Sprinkle the cheese over the vegetables. Fold over the tortilla, and cook the quesadilla in the skillet for about 1 minute on each side, until the quesadilla is golden brown and crispy. The quesadillas will crisp up more as they cool as well.

Once the quesadillas have cooled for about 1 minute, you can use a long, sharp knife to cut them into triangles. Keep in mind that dipping is easier with skinnier triangles, so fourths might be best for lunchboxes. Serve the quesadillas with the sour cream (if using), guacamole (if using), and salsa (if using) on the side for dipping.

The quesadillas will last 3 to 4 days in an airtight container in the refrigerator.

Notes

- If your tortilla wrap does not fold over well without cracking, moisten it slightly and warm it up a bit to soften it so that it folds over well. Alternatively, you could top 1 whole tortilla with the bean spread and other ingredients and then top it with another full tortilla prior to cooking. Cut these quesadillas into eighths.

- Pinto beans swap well for the black beans if those are what you have. You could use drained canned beans if you want. I keep bags of cooked beans in the freezer so I can scoop out what I want easily.

Chinese Takeout Sweet and Sour Chicken Wraps

(dairy-free option, gluten-free, nut-free, soy-free)

Sweet, savory, and satisfying, this sweet and sour look-alike is everything you love about takeout without the heavy doses of sugar, soy, and other preservatives. The whole fruit–sweetened sweet and sour sauce won't leave your little ones with sky-rocketing blood sugars—only steady, even energy balanced in a protein- and fat-packed wrap to refuel for the afternoon at school.

Makes 9 (1-cup [240-g]) servings of stir-fry; you'll use about 1 cup (240 g) of stir-fry per full wrap, but note that smaller children will eat about ½ cup (120 g) of stir-fry in ½ of a wrap

Sweet and Sour Sauce
½ cup (120 ml) fresh orange juice

3 Medjool or 6 Deglet Noor dates, pitted

1½ tbsp (23 ml) white wine vinegar

1 tbsp (17 g) tomato paste

1 tsp potato, arrowroot, or tapioca starch (do not use potato flour)

½ tsp sea salt

Stir-Fry
½ cup (80 g) potato, arrowroot, or tapioca starch (do not use potato flour)

1 tsp sea salt, plus more as needed

3 cups (420 g) cubed cooked chicken (see Notes)

1 large egg, whisked

6 tbsp (90 g) butter or ghee or 6 tbsp (90 ml) olive or avocado oil, divided

1 medium onion, cut into thin strips

2 medium bell peppers (any color), cut into thin strips

2 cups (270 g) sugar snap peas, cut in half

4 cloves garlic, minced

1 cup (165 g) finely chopped fresh, drained and canned, or thawed and drained frozen pineapple

To make the sweet and sour sauce, combine the orange juice, dates, vinegar, tomato paste, potato starch, and sea salt in a high-speed blender. Blend until the ingredients are smooth. Set the sauce aside.

To make the stir-fry, heat a large skillet over medium-high heat while you prepare the ingredients. Put the potato starch and sea salt in a freezer-safe bag. Place the chicken in a large bowl and pour the egg over the chicken, stirring the chicken with a spoon to ensure it is coated in the egg. Transfer the coated chicken to the freezer-safe bag, close the bag, and shake it to coat the chicken well.

Melt 4 tablespoons (60 g) of the butter in the hot skillet and add the coated chicken. Let the chicken crisp up for about 5 minutes, stirring occasionally, until the outside of the chicken is golden brown. Remove the chicken from the skillet and set the chicken aside.

(continued)

Wraps

Thinly sliced or shredded cabbage or lettuce, as needed

Gluten-free tortillas of choice, as needed

Wipe out the skillet and set it over medium heat. Melt the remaining 2 tablespoons (30 g) of butter in the skillet. Add the onion, bell peppers, sugar peas, and additional sea salt. Cook the stir-fry for about 7 minutes, until the veggies are crisp-tender and fragrant.

Add the garlic and cook for 1 minute. Add the pineapple, chicken, and sweet and sour sauce to the skillet. Stir to combine the chicken with the sauce, until the potato starch thickens the sauce. You can add more liquid if you like it saucier, but this amount works well for a wrap.

To make the wraps, lay some cabbage on a tortilla and lay about 1 cup (240 g) of the stir-fry on top. Wrap up the tortilla and serve, or pack the wrap in the lunchbox. (If your tortilla wrap does not roll well without cracking, moisten it slightly and heat it up a bit in a warm skillet or in the microwave for 10 seconds to soften it.)

Notes

- This stir-fry is a large amount of food. We typically eat the stir-fry for dinner as a family over rice, and then we use the leftovers for the wraps—you'll get 3 to 4 wraps if you do it this way. This recipe can be doubled for larger families.

- You can use leftover chicken from dinner using the Prep-Day Whole Chicken Two Ways recipe (page 164).

- You can use 1 pound (450 g) of uncooked chicken for this recipe. Coat the chicken the same in the egg and starch, and then cook it in the skillet for 7 to 10 minutes, making sure the chicken is cooked all the way through before proceeding with the recipe.

Restaurant-Style Club Sandwich Skewers with Awesome Sauce Dip

(dairy-free, egg-free option, gluten-free, nut-free, soy-free)

For many kids, presentation is everything. And while I don't consider myself a "Pinterest mom," there is definitely value in making lunchboxes look fun. Imagine their faces as, after a long morning at school, they open up their lunchboxes to these colorful sandwich skewers! Nothing fancy or difficult about the prep here—just their favorite sandwich ingredients with a delicious dipping sauce worthy of the name Awesome Sauce.

Makes 8 (6-inch [15-cm]) sandwich skewers

Skewers

2 to 3 slices gluten-free bread, cut into 2-inch (5-cm) squares

2 to 3 lettuce leaves, cut into 2-inch (5-cm) pieces

2 to 3 strips cooked bacon, cut into 1- to 2-inch (2.5- to 5-cm) pieces (see Notes)

1 small salad cucumber, cut into ribbons

3 to 4 slices deli meat of choice (such as Applegate Organics® brand), cut into ribbons

Cheese of choice, cut into 8 cubes (optional)

8 cherry tomatoes

Awesome Sauce Dip

½ cup (110 g) mayonnaise (such as Easy Homemade Mayo Two Ways [page 159] or store-bought avocado or olive oil mayo like Sir Kensington's brand)

¼ cup (68 g) ketchup

1 tsp onion powder

1 tsp mustard powder

Sea salt, as needed

Black pepper, as needed

Make the skewers using eight 6-inch (15-cm) blunt-edge wooden skewers to thread the bread, lettuce, bacon, cucumber, deli meat, cheese (if using), and tomatoes onto the skewers however you desire—try alternating the ingredients to make them eye-catching! (To thread the cucumber and deli meat ribbons, fold them over, making an S shape, before sliding them onto the skewers.)

To make the Awesome Sauce Dip, mix together the mayonnaise, ketchup, onion powder, and mustard powder in a medium bowl. Season the dip with the sea salt and black pepper to taste. Store the Awesome Sauce Dip in a condiment container for the lunchboxes.

Notes

- If you are egg-free, see my homemade mayo recipe on page 159 for an egg-free option.
- Cook the bacon so that it is not overly crispy to ensure that it will go on the skewers without crumbling. Let the bacon cool on a paper towel to drain the extra grease.

Brain-Boosting Egg Salad Pitas

(dairy-free, gluten-free, nut-free, soy-free)

Change up your sandwich routine with nutrient-packed egg salad! This protein-rich pita filling satiates that midday hunger, and the omega-3 fatty acids and choline found in pastured eggs boost brain function.

Makes 3 to 4 full pita pockets (depending on the pitas' size; smaller children will eat ¼ to ½ of a pita pocket, while older children will eat a full pita)

6 hard-boiled large eggs (page 162), peeled

⅓ cup (73 g) mayonnaise (such as Easy Homemade Mayo Two Ways [page 159] or store-bought avocado or olive oil mayo like Sir Kensington's or Primal Kitchen brands)

2 tsp (10 g) yellow mustard

4 green onions, finely chopped (optional)

Sea salt, as needed

Black pepper, as needed

4 to 5 lettuce leaves

3 gluten-free pita breads (such as Sami's Bakery brand)

1 medium red, yellow, or orange bell pepper, cut into thin strips

In a small bowl, combine the eggs, mayonnaise, and mustard. Use a fork to mash and stir the ingredients to reach your preferred consistency (you can make the egg pieces as small or large as you like). Fold in the green onions (if using) and season the egg salad with the sea salt and black pepper to taste.

Lay a lettuce leaf inside the bottom of a pita, then place the bell pepper strips on top of the lettuce. Spoon in the egg salad, then lay another lettuce leaf on top of the egg salad.

Slice the pita into the size that fits your lunchbox. Consider small hands as well—sometimes making smaller pita sandwiches makes it easier for little kids to pick them up and eat them.

Egg salad keeps in the refrigerator in an airtight container for 3 days.

Notes

- There are so many ways to stuff that pita to change things up. Slices of cheese, broccoli sprouts, bacon, and fermented veggies are some options.

- You could cut the pita bread into triangles and pack the egg salad in a leakproof container that comes with your lunchbox, so that your children can use the pita triangles as "scoops" for the egg salad. Toddlers and smaller children enjoy dipping, so this is a good option for them. The flatbreads from the Pizza Lunchables® Copycat recipe (page 34) work well for scooping egg salad too.

Fun Friday Pizza Paninis

(egg-free, gluten-free option, nut-free, soy-free)

Wrap up a productive school week and kick off the weekend with this fun twist on pizza day at school! These crispy pizza paninis can be made in advance on a prep day and wrapped up to make lunch-packing on Friday a breeze. Pile on your children's favorite toppings—they'll never miss that cafeteria pizza.

Makes 4 pizza paninis (young children will probably eat ½ of a panini)

3 tbsp (45 g) ghee, butter, or coconut oil or 3 tbsp (45 ml) avocado oil

1 medium onion, cut into thin strips

1 medium red, orange, or yellow bell pepper, cut into thin strips

5 white button or cremini mushrooms, thinly sliced

4 tbsp (60 g) butter

8 slices bread of choice

¼ cup (60 ml) pizza sauce

1 cup (120 g) shredded cheese of choice (see Notes)

Sliced pepperoni, as needed

In a large skillet over medium-high heat, melt the ghee. Add the onion, bell pepper, and mushrooms and cook them for 15 to 20 minutes, stirring occasionally, until the onion is golden brown and the veggies are fragrant and caramelized. Set the vegetables aside.

Preheat a panini maker to medium-high heat or a medium skillet over medium-high heat while you prepare the paninis.

Spread about ½ tablespoon (8 g) of the butter on each slice of bread. Flip the slices over so that the unbuttered side is facing up. Spoon about 1 tablespoon (15 ml) of the pizza sauce onto each slice of bread. Top the sauce with the cheese, pepperoni, and caramelized veggies. Add another sprinkle of cheese and place another slice of bread, buttered side up, on top (that is, the buttered sides of the bread should be facing outward).

Cook the paninis in the panini maker for 3 minutes or in the skillet for 2 to 3 minutes on each side (press the sandwiches down if you are using a skillet), until the bread is golden brown and crispy and the cheese is melted.

The paninis will keep in an airtight container in the refrigerator for 3 days.

Notes

- The veggies can be cooked in advance on a prep day so that they are quick to add to the paninis.
- Goat cheese works well if you can't tolerate cow's milk cheese.

Lunchables® Copycats

Put the kids in the driver's seat as they pick and choose how to build their own lunches!

I remember the first time my oldest came home from kindergarten, telling me about a friend at school bringing "the coolest" lunch to school that day. Her eyes were wide with excitement as she told me about how her friend got to make her very own little pizzas with this "new" lunch called Lunchables®. When the amazement continued a few days later as this same friend got to make her very own cracker sandwiches with cheese and turkey, it dawned on me: "Wait a minute, I can do that!"

The Lunchables® idea is fantastic. Kids love to be in charge of their food. With a few swaps to include fresher ingredient choices and a few tweaks (like making quick pizza flatbreads out of healthier flour), we can re-create this fun lunch concept in a real-food way that will keep kids nourished for the long school afternoon—and they can have a little fun while they're at it! Your kids will be the ones running home and saying how fun it was to build their own cracker sandwiches, fun yogurt parfaits, and even their own BLTs.

How to Pack These Lunchables® Copycats for a Balanced Lunchbox

All of the Lunchables® Copycat concepts in this chapter are a good source of protein and fat. When I make these recipes for my kids, I'm typically just adding an easy side of fruit and veggies, making prep for these lunchboxes even easier. Use whatever fresh fruit and vegetables are in season near you. Salads or leftover dinner veggies are also easy options. In the middle of winter when fresh fruit is expensive or hard to come by, I use dried fruits (just watch the ingredient labels to avoid added sugar).

Pizza Lunchables® Copycat

(dairy-free option, egg-free, gluten-free, nut-free, soy-free)

Filled with nourishing, real ingredients, this is the perfect copycat of a Lunchables® pizza that you can feel good about treating the kids to. The no-fuss, prebiotic-rich cassava flour flatbreads are fast to make, and they are great to make on prep day and freeze.

Makes 10 mini pizza flatbreads

Cassava Flour Flatbreads

1¼ cups (175 g) cassava flour

1 tsp aluminum-free baking powder

1 tbsp (12 g) organic cane sugar or turbinado sugar

1 tsp onion powder

¼ tsp garlic powder

Pinch of sea salt

1 tbsp (15 ml) olive oil

2 tsp (10 ml) apple cider vinegar

1 cup (240 ml) water

Pizza Lunchables®

Pizza sauce, as needed

Shredded cheese of choice, as needed (see Notes)

Sliced olives, as needed

Diced bell peppers (any color), as needed

Sliced pepperoni or crumbled cooked sausage, as needed

To make the cassava flour flatbreads, preheat a medium skillet over medium-high heat while you mix the dough. (Do not oil the skillet.)

In a small bowl, mix together the flour, baking powder, sugar, onion powder, garlic powder, sea salt, oil, vinegar, and water. Mix the ingredients until the dough comes together (I start with a spatula and finish with my hands).

Pinch off about 10 balls of dough for the flatbreads. You can make them smaller or bigger if you wish.

Using your hands, roll and then flatten the pieces of dough into discs that are ¼ inch (6 mm) thick and 3 to 6 inches (7.5 to 15 cm) in diameter. Place them in the hot skillet. Cook the flatbreads for 1 to 2 minutes, until they are golden brown. Flip the flatbreads over and cook them for about 1 minute. Transfer them to a plate or baking rack to cool. To freeze the flatbreads, let them cool completely and store them flat in a freezer-safe bag. You can put them into the lunchboxes frozen and they'll thaw by lunchtime.

To make the pizza Lunchables®, assemble the lunchbox with the flatbreads and the pizza toppings that your child enjoys, such as the pizza sauce, cheese, olives, bell peppers, and pepperoni.

Notes

- This is a very basic flatbread recipe—I enjoy adding about 1 teaspoon of Italian seasoning for extra flavor. If your children are used to a sweeter flatbread, you can bump up the sugar a bit. I don't recommend using honey, as it tends to burn.

- Dairy-free kids that can handle goat cheese will love using a spoon for spreadable goat cheese on their flatbreads.

Build Your Own Mexican Nachos

(dairy-free option, egg-free, gluten-free, nut-free, soy-free)

The kids will be so excited to fill up their favorite tortillas with these fun Mexican-inspired ingredients. You'll gladly let them pile on the refried beans for a budget-friendly protein boost, and I've got the secret to a heat-free guacamole that even your toughest spice critic will adore—I know because I have one living with me!

Makes 3 cups (720 g) refried beans and 2 cups (460 g) guacamole

Refried Beans

2 to 3 tbsp (30 to 45 g) butter, ghee, or coconut oil or 2 to 3 tbsp (30 to 45 ml) avocado oil

1 small onion, finely chopped

1 tsp plus a pinch of sea salt, divided

3 cloves garlic, minced

2 cups (340 g) sprouted canned or home-cooked pinto beans (page 163), drained and rinsed if needed

1½ tsp (5 g) ground cumin

1 tsp paprika

¼ tsp chili powder

½ tsp black pepper

⅓ cup (80 ml) full-fat coconut milk or whole milk

Guacamole

½ medium onion, diced

1 medium tomato, diced

Juice of ½ small lime

2 medium avocados, pitted and cubed

1 to 2 tsp (3 to 6 g) garlic powder

Sea salt, to taste

To make the refried beans, melt the butter in a medium saucepan over medium heat. Add the onion and a pinch of sea salt and sauté the onion for 5 minutes.

Add the garlic and cook for 1 minute, then add the pinto beans, remaining 1 teaspoon of sea salt, cumin, paprika, chili powder, black pepper, and coconut milk. Stir everything together, and bring the beans to a low simmer, reducing the heat as necessary to maintain the simmer. Cook them for 10 minutes, stirring occasionally, until the milk is absorbed.

Use a potato masher to mash the beans or an immersion blender to blend them. Alternatively, you can transfer the beans to a traditional blender and blend them until they are completely smooth.

The refried beans will keep for 1 week in the refrigerator. To freeze the refried beans, cool them completely and transfer them to a freezer-safe container for storage.

To make the guacamole, combine the onion, tomato, lime juice, avocados, and garlic powder in a medium bowl. Use a fork to mix all of the ingredients together. Depending on the texture that your kids enjoy, you can leave the guacamole chunky or you can use the back of the fork to mash the avocado to a smoother consistency. Some kids may even enjoy the guacamole blended up in the food processor until it is completely smooth.

Taste the guacamole and season it with the sea salt to taste. Store the guacamole in a sealed pint-size (475-ml) Mason jar in the refrigerator for 2 to 3 days.

(continued)

Build Your Own Mexican Nachos (cont.)

Mexican Fiesta Lunchbox

Gluten-free tortillas or tortilla chips, as needed

Shredded cheese, as needed (optional)

Full-fat sour cream, as needed (optional)

Diced bell peppers (any color), as needed

Sliced olives, as needed

To assemble the Mexican Fiesta Lunchbox, pack some tortillas in one compartment and the refried beans, guacamole, cheese (if using), sour cream (if using), bell peppers, and olives in separate compartments (to minimize browning in the guacamole, pack it in a leakproof condiment container). The kids can pile their tortillas with the refried beans, guacamole, cheese, sour cream, bell peppers, olives, or whatever they love. If you have young children that might not have the time or skill to make their own, you can make their tortillas for them and let them dip the rolled-up tortillas into the guacamole.

Note

- If your little one feels like onions are "spicy" in guacamole, swap the fresh onion for 1 to 2 teaspoons (3 to 6 g) of onion powder. Fresh garlic tends to add a spicy bite to guacamole, which is why the garlic powder works so well in this recipe.

Easy Homemade Cracker Stackers Lunchables® Copycat

(dairy-free option, egg-free, gluten-free, nut-free, soy-free)

This is where it all began! My daughter was determined to have a fun lunch like her friends, and I wanted her to have that too. It is so empowering to look at something from the store and know that you can duplicate it yourself. While I'm all for a quality store-bought cracker, many of the "healthier" boxed crackers are either full of nuts that nut-free school zones cannot have, are really pricey, or are made with cheaper oils that aren't healthy to consume on a regular basis. These easy, budget-friendly, nut-free crackers are salty and slightly sweet, and they keep in the pantry just as well as any store-bought cracker.

Makes 30 (2-inch [5-cm]-diameter) crackers

Crackers

1 cup (122 g) Namaste Perfect Flour Blend, plus more as needed

¼ cup (60 g) cold butter or palm shortening, cut into 4 to 6 slices

1 tsp raw honey

¼ tsp sea salt, plus more as needed

¼ cup (60 ml) water, plus more as needed

To make the crackers, preheat the oven to 400°F (204°C). Line a large baking sheet with a silicone baking mat or unbleached parchment paper.

Put the flour, butter, honey, and salt in a food processor and process until the butter is broken up into small pieces within the flour.

With the food processor running, pour the water through the hole in the top of the processor and let the dough process until it comes together in a ball. If a ball of dough does not come together within 30 seconds, add 1 tablespoon (15 ml) of water at a time until it does.

Dust a work surface with flour. Roll the dough as thin as you can—about ⅛ inch (3 mm) or thinner. Use a small cookie cutter to cut the desired shape of cracker. Place the crackers on the prepared baking sheet. You can re-roll any leftover dough for more crackers. If desired, sprinkle the tops of the crackers with additional sea salt.

Bake the crackers for 13 to 14 minutes, until the bottoms are golden brown. Turn the oven off and keep the crackers in the oven for 10 to 11 minutes to allow them to become crisp without overcooking. Take the crackers out of the oven and let them cool completely (they will crisp up completely once they are cool).

(continued)

Easy Homemade Cracker Stackers
Lunchables® Copycat (cont.)

Cracker Stackers Lunchables®

Deli meat sliced into roughly the size of the crackers, as needed

Cheese sliced into roughly the size of the crackers, as needed (optional)

To make the Cracker Stackers Lunchables®, put the crackers, deli meat, and cheese (if using) near each other but separated so that the crackers do not get soggy. Silicone cups or muffin cups work well if you need divided compartments.

You can add fresh or dried fruit and veggies to other compartments of the lunchbox to make it a balanced meal.

Note

- I have a 2-inch (5-cm) scalloped edge circle cutter that makes these crackers look like a RITZ cracker in shape, but any size cutter will do. Smaller crackers do take less time to bake, so reduce the baking time to 10 minutes and the oven-off time to 7 minutes. Also, keep in mind that the 2-inch (5-cm) size makes for easier stacking than smaller crackers do.

Breakfast-for-Lunch
"Brunchables®" Copycat
(dairy-free, gluten-free, nut-free, soy-free)

Make your Saturday morning pancake breakfast work double time for you! The softest, fluffiest pancakes you've ever seen, and kid-approved mild breakfast sausages sized perfectly for little hands pack easily into lunchboxes after your weekend breakfast. Since this recipe is made with clean ingredients that won't send blood sugars soaring, you can feel good about packing a fun breakfast-for-lunch Brunchables®.

Makes 65 to 70 mini pancake dippers and 35 to 40 mini sausage patties

Pancakes

2 large eggs, yolks and whites separated, divided

1½ cups (360 ml) full-fat coconut milk or whole milk

1 tbsp (15 ml) apple cider vinegar

2 tbsp (24 g) coconut sugar or maple sugar, or 2 tbsp (30 ml) pure maple syrup

2 tbsp (30 ml) olive oil, plus more as needed

1 cup (140 g) Otto's brand cassava flour

2 tsp (8 g) aluminum-free baking powder

½ tsp sea salt

Ground cinnamon, as needed (optional)

To make the pancakes, beat the 2 egg whites in a medium bowl until they are fluffy and form stiff peaks, about 1 minute. Set the egg whites aside.

In a medium bowl, whisk together the egg yolks, milk, vinegar, sugar, and oil until the mixture is smooth.

Add the cassava flour, baking powder, sea salt, and cinnamon (if using). Stir to combine the ingredients until they are smooth, then fold in the whipped egg whites. Avoid overmixing so that the egg whites will keep the batter fluffy.

Heat a medium skillet over medium-high heat. Pour a little additional oil into the skillet. Add about 1 tablespoon (15 ml) of batter to the skillet for each pancake. (You could also make long oval dippers or whatever shape you like.) Cook the pancakes for about 1 minute, until there are a few bubbles on the top. Flip the pancakes and cook them for about 1 minute on the other side. The pancakes should be golden brown on each side. Transfer the pancakes to a baking rack to cool.

(continued)

Breakfast-for-Lunch
"Brunchables®" Copycat (cont.)

Sausages

1 tbsp (15 g) butter or 1 tbsp (15 ml) olive oil

1 lb (450 g) ground pork or turkey

1 tsp onion powder

1 tsp garlic powder

½ tsp dried basil

½ tsp dried thyme

¼ tsp ground cumin

¼ tsp dried marjoram

1 tsp sea salt

⅛ to ¼ tsp black pepper

Brunchables® Lunchbox

Pure maple syrup, as needed

To make the sausages, melt the butter in a large skillet over medium-high heat. While the butter melts, mix together the pork, onion powder, garlic powder, basil, thyme, cumin, marjoram, sea salt, and black pepper in a medium bowl.

Scoop out 1-tablespoon (15-g) portions of the sausage mixture and form little sausage patties or links with your hands. Place them in the hot skillet, being careful not to overcrowd the skillet. Working in batches, cook the sausages for 2 to 3 minutes on each side, until they are golden brown and cooked all the way through. (The exact cooking time will vary based on the size of the sausages you make.)

To build the Brunchables® Lunchbox, pour the maple syrup into a condiment container and place it in the lunchbox. Place the mini pancakes next to the condiment container of syrup and the sausages in a separate compartment.

Add sides of fruit and veggies to balance the lunchbox.

Notes

- You can serve your pancake dippers in the lunchbox with maple syrup in the condiment container, or you can cook down some fresh or frozen fruit to make a fruit dip—add a drizzle of honey or maple syrup if the fruit isn't sweet enough.

- To freeze the pancake dippers and mini sausages, let them cool completely and then store them flat in freezer-safe bags. You can pull them from the freezer and place them right in the lunchboxes and they will thaw by lunchtime!

- The sausage recipe is kid-friendly mild. If you like some heat in your breakfast sausage, try adding ¼ to ½ teaspoon of cayenne pepper to the sausage mixture.

Build Your Own
Nourishing Yogurt Parfait
(dairy-free, egg-free, gluten-free, nut-free option, soy-free)

What is the point of eating "healthy" granola if it is cooked in an unhealthy fat and loaded with sugar? Now you can replace pricey, sugary store-bought granola with your own crispy, crunchy, honey-sweetened granola lightly baked in nourishing fat to fuel busy, growing bodies. Add a side of mixed berries and control the sweetness with a fun honey swirl, and the kids can build their own parfait that is sure to keep them focused for the rest of the school day.

Makes 14 cups (1.1 kg) granola

Granola
5 cups (400 g) rolled oats (not quick oats)

2 cups (224 g) seeds and/or nuts, coarsely chopped (see Note)

½ cup (89 g) buckwheat groats

½ cup (100 g) hulled millet

¼ cup (86 g) chia seeds

¼ cup (43 g) flaxseed meal

½ tsp sea salt (if using unsalted seeds and/or nuts; optional)

¼ cup (48 g) coconut sugar

½ cup (120 g) coconut oil

¾ cup (180 ml) raw honey or pure maple syrup

1 tbsp (15 ml) pure vanilla extract

1 tsp ground cinnamon (optional)

Raw cacao nibs, as needed (optional)

Dried fruit (such as raisins, apples, chopped figs, or blueberries), as needed (optional)

To make the granola, preheat the oven to 325°F (163°C). Set out two large baking sheets, but do not line or grease them.

In a large bowl, combine the oats, seeds and/or nuts, buckwheat groats, millet, chia seeds, flaxseed meal, sea salt (if using), and sugar. Set the oat mixture aside.

Melt the oil in a small saucepan over medium heat. Turn off the heat and stir in the honey and vanilla.

Add the oil mixture to the oat mixture, add the cinnamon (if using), and stir to combine well.

Spread the granola mixture onto the baking sheets. Bake the granola for 10 minutes. Stir the mixture and bake it for 10 minutes. Stir the mixture one more time and bake for 10 more minutes. Remove the baking sheets from the oven and let the granola cool completely. It will crisp up as it cools.

After the granola has cooled, add the raw cacao nibs (if using) and dried fruit (if using).

Store the cooled granola in an airtight container in the pantry.

(continued)

Nourishing Yogurt Parfait

Full-fat yogurt or coconut yogurt, as needed

Raw honey, as needed (optional)

Berries of choice, as needed

To assemble the Nourishing Yogurt Parfait, use a leakproof container for packing the yogurt and add a drizzle of honey (if using).

Pack the granola in a side compartment that your child can pick up and pour into the yogurt. The berries can be packed in a separate side compartment.

Note

- If you are nut-free or at a nut-free school, you can use raw pumpkin seeds, raw unsalted sunflower seeds, sesame seeds, flaxseed, or hemp seeds. I love the combo of sunflower and pumpkin seeds. If you tolerate nuts and can have them at school, try a combination of nuts and seeds to add a variety of nutrients.

"Charcuterie Board" Lunchbox

(egg-free option, gluten-free, nut-free option, soy-free)

When my girls are home from school, hands down their favorite type of meal is charcuterie board–style eating. We eat this fun, family-style meal most weeks of the summer, and when school starts, it is fun to pack their lunchboxes this way every once in a while. Most kids love little bits and bites of food to stack, dip, spread, and munch! Blend up this quick, kid-friendly pesto for their crackers and veggie sticks, and throw in some side items like fresh or dried fruit, nuts or seeds, olives, cheese, summer sausage, deli meat, and hard-boiled eggs to make an interactive, appealing board-style lunch.

Makes 1 cup (252 g) pesto

Pesto

2 cups (48 g) packed fresh basil leaves

Heaping ⅓ cup (40 g) walnuts or raw unsalted sunflower seeds (see Notes)

½ cup (60 g) shredded firm raw cheese (see Notes)

¼ tsp sea salt, or to taste

Pinch of black pepper

1 clove garlic or ¼ to ½ tsp garlic powder

½ cup (120 ml) olive oil

"Charcuterie Board" Lunchbox

Gluten-free crackers, as needed

Veggie sticks, as needed

Olives, as needed

Nuts or seeds, as needed

Cheese squares, as needed (optional)

Sliced deli meat or summer sausage, as needed

Sliced hard-boiled pastured eggs, as needed (optional)

Fresh or dried fruit, as needed

To make the pesto, put the basil leaves and walnuts in a food processor and pulse a few times to combine them.

Add the cheese, sea salt, black pepper, and garlic. Pulse several times, until everything is very small and well combined.

With the food processor running, slowly drizzle in the oil through the hole in the top of the food processor. This will allow the oil to emulsify, thickening the pesto.

To assemble the "Charcuterie Board" Lunchbox, pack the pesto in a leakproof container for dipping.

Use separate compartments to pack the crackers, veggie sticks, olives, nuts or seeds, cheese (if using), deli meat, hard-boiled eggs (if using), and fruit, mixing and matching the ingredients according to your child's preferences. (I like to use little silicone cups or muffin cups for separating compartments further if needed.)

Notes

- If you have access to pine nuts, use ⅓ cup (45 g) of them for the pesto. Pine nuts are the more traditional ingredient in pesto. I don't have access to quality pine nuts, so I tend to use organic walnuts.
- Manchego or a hard goat cheese works if you can have sheep's or goat's milk.

Build Your Own BLT Lunchables® with Amazin' Bacon Dipping Sauce

(gluten-free, nut-free, soy-free, egg-free)

I'm pretty sure anything with bacon will get any kid through an otherwise mundane middle-of-the-week school day! Put a smile on their faces with BLTs that they get to make themselves. They'll swoon over my super special Amazin' Bacon Dipping Sauce, and you can feel good about a lunch filled with nourishing, satiating ingredients that will fuel them for the afternoon.

Makes about 2 cups (480 ml) Amazin' Bacon Dipping Sauce

Amazin' Bacon Dipping Sauce

⅓ cup (80 ml) avocado or olive oil

2 tbsp (30 g) bacon grease

½ cup (60 g) full-fat sour cream

2 tsp (10 ml) white wine vinegar or distilled white vinegar

1 tbsp (15 ml) raw honey

¼ tsp garlic powder

Salt, as needed

BLT Lunchables®

Gluten-free pita breads, cut into triangles, as needed

Lettuce leaves, cut to fit the pita triangles, as needed

Sliced tomato, as needed

Cooked bacon strips, as needed

To make the Amazin' Bacon Dipping Sauce, combine the oil, bacon grease, sour cream, vinegar, honey, garlic powder, and salt in a large bowl. Blend the ingredients with an immersion blender until they are smooth and creamy. Store the sauce in a lidded jar in the refrigerator for up to 1 week.

To make the BLT Lunchables®, arrange the pita breads, lettuce leaves, tomato, and bacon in the lunchbox so that your child can build their sandwich easily. Place the Amazin' Bacon Dipping Sauce in a condiment container with an airtight lid. Alternatively, build the pitas yourself, and use blunt-edge toothpicks to hold the mini sandwiches together—this method might work well for little ones who will struggle with the time management of building their own sandwich during the time constraints of a school lunch.

Notes

- If you are building the sandwiches on toothpicks, it would be best to keep the bacon cooked soft so it does not crumble when you skewer it.
- The Amazin' Bacon Dipping Sauce works well on salads too!

Warm and Comforting
Thermos Lunches

Bring some calm to the kids' busy school day with warm bowls of comfort at lunchtime! There is nothing quite like taking a break with a bowl of warm and cozy food on a busy day. Bone broth–based soups were one of the very first whole-food recipes I learned to make in my real-food journey when my girls were babies, so I wanted to send a little piece of our warm home with them to school every once in a while. Their Tuesday and Thursday thermos days are looked forward to weekly as they eagerly ask what "warm lunch" they get to have that week. See page 165 for my recipe for homemade bone broth, and tips for incorporating this nourishing food into your weekly or monthly meal prep.

Round out your lunchbox menu rotation in no time with nutrient-dense spins on kid-friendly classics like Comforting Beef Noodle Soup (page 54) and cozy kid favorites like The Creamiest, Dreamiest Broccoli Cheese Soup (page 62) and perfect-for-grilled-cheese-dunking Creamy Tomato Bisque (page 57). And you're sure to get smiles when they open their thermoses of fun childhood copycats like a whole-food version of SpaghettiOs® (page 58) and a mac 'n' cheese look-alike without the dairy (page 61)!

How to Pack Nourishing Thermos Lunches for a Balanced Lunchbox and How to Use a Lunchbox Thermos

When packing lunchbox thermoses, use a smaller bento box to pack the side items to go with the soup or meal. Depending on the protein and fat content of the thermos lunch, you'll want to either add just a simple fruit, veggie, or salad side if the thermos lunch is a full meal—like the Comforting Beef Noodle Soup (page 54)—or you can add an easy sandwich or a combination of crackers, cheese, and meat with some fruit if you pack a veggie-based soup to make sure there is some filling protein and fat.

Temper your thermos with hot water from your tap before filling it with the hot soup, so that the cold thermos doesn't cool off your warm meal. Be sure to pack a spoon for scoopable meals, or include a straw for mess-free soup slurping!

Comforting Beef Noodle Soup

(dairy-free, egg-free, gluten-free, nut-free, soy-free)

This warm and comforting hearty lunch is a new spin on the classic chicken noodle soup! Whether you use your Sunday dinner beef roast leftovers or brown up some grass-fed ground beef especially for lunches, this pot of soup is easy enough to make on a Monday night and pack up the leftovers into thermoses for school later in the week.

Makes 8 to 10 cups (1.9 to 2.4 L) soup

3 to 4 tbsp (45 to 60 g) butter or 3 to 4 tbsp (45 to 60 ml) olive oil

1 medium onion, diced

8 oz (227 g) white button or cremini mushrooms, thickly or thinly sliced

2 large carrots, peeled and diced

2 ribs celery, diced

Sea salt, as needed

3 cloves garlic, minced

10 cups (2.4 L) bone broth (page 165)

2 cups (300 g) shredded leftover grass-fed beef roast or ½ lb (225 g) grass-fed ground beef, browned

1 tsp dried oregano

1 tsp dried basil

3 cups (345 g) uncooked gluten-free pasta of choice (such as Jovial brand gluten-free rice pasta)

Black pepper, as needed

Melt the butter in a large soup pot over medium heat. Add the onion, mushrooms, carrots, and celery. Add a big pinch of sea salt and cook the vegetables for 10 minutes, stirring every 2 minutes, until the veggies are soft and golden in color.

Add the garlic and cook for 1 minute.

Add the broth, beef, oregano, and basil and increase the heat to high. Bring the soup to a boil. Add the pasta and cook the soup until the pasta is al dente or to your liking. The pasta will continue to absorb the liquid for up to 10 minutes after turning the heat off, so do not let the pasta cook too long. Season the soup with sea salt and black pepper to taste.

This soup will last 3 to 4 days in the refrigerator.

Notes

- Traditional spaghetti-style pasta seen in most chicken noodle soups can be tough for little ones to manage without making a mess at school, especially when they are scooping spoonfuls out of a thermos versus a bowl like they would at home. I have found using smaller noodle shapes like bow tie, elbow macaroni, shells, or spirals are much easier for my younger kids to handle at school.

- I love to add chopped spinach to this soup to wilt in after the pasta cooks. It adds some pretty (and taste-free!) color. It is a great way to use up spinach that is starting to wilt and bump up the veggie component to the soup at the same time.

Creamy Tomato Bisque

(dairy-free option, egg-free, gluten-free, nut-free, soy-free)

There is nothing more comforting on a snowy afternoon or a drizzly day than a warm bowl of tomato soup and grilled cheese. A fantastic way to introduce bone broth into your little one's diet, tomato soup is an easy kid-favorite flavor they will ask for over and over again! Be sure to check out the Fun and Fast Grilled Cheese Dunkers on page 91 for a fun twist on grilled cheese sandwiches to go with your tomato bisque!

Makes 14 cups (3.4 L) soup

3 tbsp (45 g) butter, divided (see Notes)

2 tbsp (30 ml) olive oil

2 medium onions, coarsely chopped

2 medium carrots, coarsely chopped

Sea salt, as needed

3 cloves garlic, coarsely chopped

2 tbsp (34 g) tomato paste

5 large ripe tomatoes, seeds removed and coarsely chopped (see Notes)

6 cups (1.4 L) bone broth (page 165)

¼ cup (6 g) loosely packed fresh basil leaves or 1 tbsp (3 g) dried basil

¼ cup (60 ml) full-fat coconut milk, raw milk, or cream

1 to 2 tbsp (15 to 30 ml) raw honey (see Notes)

Black pepper, as needed

In a large soup pot over medium-high heat, melt 2 tablespoons (30 g) of the butter and the oil. Add the onions, carrots, and a pinch of sea salt. Cook the vegetables for 10 minutes, until they are soft and golden.

Add the garlic and tomato paste and cook the mixture for 2 minutes, until the garlic is fragrant and the tomato paste has incorporated into the veggies.

Add the tomatoes, broth, and basil leaves, and bring the soup to a simmer. Cook for 20 minutes, until the tomatoes are very soft and almost falling apart.

Turn the heat off and add the milk, honey, and the remaining 1 tablespoon (15 g) of butter. Use an immersion blender to puree the soup until it is smooth and creamy. (Alternatively, blend the soup with a countertop blender, working in batches if necessary.) Season the soup with sea salt and black pepper to taste.

This soup freezes very well. Take advantage of summer tomatoes and fresh basil and load your freezer up! To freeze, cool the soup completely and store it in freezer-safe containers.

Notes

- If you are dairy-free, ghee replaces the butter well if you can have that, or you can use all olive or avocado oil.
- You can use 2 (32-ounce [896-g]) cans of whole tomatoes.
- The honey is to cut the acidity of the tomatoes. Very ripe, summer-sweet, vine-ripened tomatoes may only need a few teaspoons of honey.

Kid-Favorite SpaghettiOs® Copycat
(dairy-free option, egg-free, gluten-free, nut-free, soy-free)

My oldest was three years old when she saw a can of Elmo-shaped SpaghettiOs® at the grocery store, and she just had to have it. Of course, high-fructose corn syrup and a load of preservatives were not on my list of must-have foods to put in my toddler—so we figured out quickly how to make our own version with the same flavor and fun shapes. The buttery sautéed veggies naturally release a sweetness to the sauce that rivals the canned version without shooting kids' blood sugar sky-high. And they will love the taste!

Makes about 10 (1-cup [200-g]) servings

1 lb (450 g) uncooked gluten-free pasta of choice (see Notes)

3 tbsp (45 g) butter or ghee or 3 tbsp (45 ml) olive or avocado oil

1 small onion, coarsely chopped

2 carrots, peeled and coarsely chopped

1 rib celery, coarsely chopped

Sea salt, as needed

2 cloves garlic, coarsely chopped

1 tbsp (17 g) tomato paste

3 (15-oz [450-ml]) cans tomato sauce

1 tbsp (15 ml) honey

½ cup (120 ml) starchy pasta cooking water

Black pepper, as needed

Bring a large pot of water to a boil over high heat. Add the pasta and cook it until it is just shy of al dente (that is, a few minutes shy of the package directions). Be sure to reserve ½ cup (120 ml) of the starchy pasta water before you strain your cooked pasta.

While the pasta cooks, melt the butter in a large saucepan over medium heat. Add the onion, carrots, celery, and a few pinches of sea salt and cook the vegetables for about 10 minutes, until they are soft.

Add the garlic and tomato paste and cook the mixture for 1 to 2 minutes. Add the tomato sauce and honey. Bring the mixture to a low simmer. Cook it for about 10 minutes.

Add the starchy pasta cooking water to the sauce and use an immersion blender to puree the sauce. (Alternatively, you can blend the sauce in a countertop blender, working in batches if necessary.) Add the cooked pasta to the sauce, and season it with sea salt and black pepper to taste. You could add more water or some bone broth if you want a runnier sauce.

Notes

- I like the Jovial or Tinkyáda® brands of gluten-free rice pastas in the shell or elbow shapes. There are some gluten-free O-shaped pastas online as well.

- The sauce can be made and frozen in portion sizes to meet the needs of your family. That way, you can make the amount of pasta that you want and add the sauce as you go. The cooked noodles and sauce do not freeze together well, so this is the best way to have it ready to go for thermoses in a pinch.

Dairy Fake-Out Mac 'n' Cheese Copycat

(dairy-free, egg-free, gluten-free, nut-free, soy-free)

Whether you are dairy-free or not, this fun and quick mac is a healthy spin on the comforting classic. In less time than it takes to boil your pasta, you'll have a creamy, dreamy fake-out cheese sauce that feels just as decadent as the dairy version. This fun thermos lunch will make them smile on an otherwise "everyday" school day!

Makes 5 (1-cup [200-g]) servings

2 tbsp (30 ml) olive oil

3 cups (345 g) uncooked gluten-free pasta of choice (see Notes)

1 cup (240 ml) full-fat coconut milk

1 tbsp (12 g) nutritional yeast

½ cup (225 g) pureed butternut squash (see Notes)

1 tbsp (10 g) potato starch (do not use potato flour)

½ tsp sea salt, plus more as needed

Black pepper, as needed

Bring a medium pot of water to a boil over high heat. Add the oil, and then stir in the pasta. Cook the pasta for about 6 minutes, until it is al dente or cooked to your preference.

While the pasta cooks, make the cheese sauce. In a medium saucepan, combine the milk, nutritional yeast, butternut squash, potato starch, and sea salt. Whisk the ingredients together, then turn the heat on to medium. Bring the sauce to a low simmer for 30 seconds, whisking continuously. The sauce will start to thicken when it begins to simmer. Turn the heat off.

Drain the pasta and return it to its pot. Add the cheese sauce and stir to combine. Season the mac 'n' cheese with sea salt and black pepper to taste.

When reheating the mac 'n' cheese for thermoses, add a splash of water to the pot as it is warming through. A little olive oil softens the noodles as well.

Notes

- We like the Jovial or Tinkyáda® brands of gluten-free rice pastas in the elbow, corkscrew, or shell shapes.
- Canned squash will work, but I love the flavor best using butternut squash that I have cooked and pureed. You can make some squash for dinner and just reserve ½ cup (225 g) for making the mac 'n' cheese, or freeze ½-cup (225-g) portions of squash so you can easily grab it when you want to make this dish.

The Creamiest, Dreamiest Broccoli Cheese Soup

(dairy-free, egg-free, gluten-free, nut-free, soy-free)

It was from dreams of Panera Bread™'s creamy broccoli soup that this recipe was born! You'll never miss the dairy in this creamy version of your favorite comforting broccoli soup. With simple prep and kid-friendly flavor, this will quickly become a dinner staple that will fill lunchbox thermoses the next day with the greatest of ease.

Makes 8 cups (1.9 L) soup

3 tbsp (45 g) ghee or 3 tbsp (45 ml) olive or avocado oil

1 large onion, diced

2 medium carrots, peeled and diced

2 medium ribs celery, diced

Sea salt, as needed

4 cloves garlic, minced

3 to 4 cups (525 to 700 g) bite-size broccoli florets

¼ cup (40 g) potato starch (do not use potato flour)

4 to 6 cups (906 ml to 1.4 L) bone broth (page 165)

1 cup (240 ml) full-fat coconut milk

Black pepper, as needed

Melt the ghee in a large soup pot over medium-high heat. Add the onion, carrots, celery, and a big pinch of sea salt. Cook the vegetables, stirring occasionally, for about 10 minutes, until the veggies are soft and starting to caramelize.

Add the garlic and cook for 1 minute. Stir in the broccoli and potato starch, making sure the potato starch is coating the veggies well.

Stir in the broth and milk and reduce the heat to medium. Bring the soup to a simmer and cook until the broccoli is tender, 3 to 5 minutes for crisp-tender broccoli and 7 to 10 minutes for softer broccoli. Season the soup with sea salt and black pepper to taste.

This soup will last for 5 days in the refrigerator, or it can be frozen in freezer-safe containers for up to 3 months.

Notes

- If you tolerate dairy, you can cook your veggies in butter and use raw milk or cream instead of the coconut milk.

- If your kids like soup purees versus pieces of vegetables in their soup, you can puree this soup completely once the broccoli is soft.

Winter Blues Buster Creamy Potato Soup

(dairy-free option, egg-free, gluten-free, nut-free, soy-free)

This is my go-to comfort soup to bring to everyone from sick friends and new mommas to hardworking teachers and, of course, my own family. When those gray skies and feet of snow have you cooped up inside, warm up with comforting bowls of this creamy broth boasting soft bites of potato and a hint of bacon flavor. These school thermoses are sure to wrap your kids in a warm hug to remind them of home on the snowiest school days!

Makes 10 to 12 cups (2.4 to 2.9 L) soup

3 tbsp (45 g) butter or ghee or 3 tbsp (45 ml) olive oil

1 tbsp (15 g) bacon grease (optional; use an additional 1 tbsp [15 g] butter or 1 tbsp [15 ml] olive oil if not using)

2 medium onions, diced

2 medium carrots, peeled and diced

2 medium ribs celery, diced

Sea salt, as needed

4 cloves garlic, minced

3 lbs (1.4 kg) yellow potatoes, cut into ½-inch (13-mm) cubes

¼ cup (38 g) white rice flour

6 cups (1.4 L) bone broth (page 165)

2 to 3 cups (60 to 90 g) baby kale or baby spinach, finely chopped

½ cup (120 ml) full-fat coconut milk (see Notes)

Black pepper, as needed

Melt the butter and bacon grease (if using) in a large soup pot over medium heat. Add the onions, carrots, celery, and a big pinch of sea salt. Cook the vegetables, stirring occasionally, for 7 to 10 minutes, until the veggies are soft and caramelized.

Add the garlic and potatoes and increase the heat to medium-high. Cook the mixture, stirring occasionally, for 10 minutes, until the potatoes are fork tender.

Stir in the rice flour, and then add the broth. Bring the soup to a simmer and cook it for 5 to 7 minutes, until the potatoes are very soft.

Turn the heat off. Ladle half of the soup into a large heatproof bowl. Use an immersion blender to completely puree the soup in the bowl. (Alternatively, you can blend the soup in a countertop blender, working in batches if necessary.) Return the pureed soup to the pot, stir to combine, and add the baby kale. Turn on the heat to medium-high and bring the soup to a simmer again for 2 to 3 minutes to wilt the kale.

Stir in the milk. Season the soup with sea salt and black pepper to taste.

This soup lasts 5 days in the refrigerator, or it can be frozen in freezer-safe containers for up to 3 months.

Notes

- If you tolerate dairy, you can replace the coconut milk with cream.
- The soup does continue to thicken a bit as it cools. When preparing the soup for thermoses, you can add more broth if you wish.

The Best Chinese Takeout Copycat

(dairy-free, egg-free, gluten-free, nut-free, soy-free)

Plan a fun fake-out takeout dinner in your dinner rotation, and then pack the leftovers into thermoses the next day or later in the week. The satisfying umami flavors of the sauce and crispy chicken feel just like the restaurant version without the soy, sugar, salt, and extra preservatives. Your kids' thermoses will be the envy of their lunch tablemates, and they will feel full and focused during the afternoon.

Makes 8 to 10 (1-cup [240-g]) servings

¼ cup (60 ml) coconut aminos

2 tbsp (30 ml) white wine vinegar

2 tbsp (30 ml) raw honey

1 tsp blackstrap molasses

5 tbsp (75 g) ghee or butter or 5 tbsp (75 ml) olive oil, divided

4 cups (560 g) cooked cubed chicken (see Note)

1 tbsp (15 ml) olive oil

¼ cup (40 g) potato starch (do not use potato flour)

1 tsp ground ginger

½ tsp sea salt, plus more as needed

1 medium onion, sliced into medium strips

1 medium red, orange, or yellow bell pepper, sliced into medium strips

4 to 6 oz (112 to 170 g) white button or cremini mushrooms, thinly sliced

3 cups (405 g) sugar snap peas

4 cloves garlic, minced

Black pepper, as needed

Cooked long-grain white rice or gluten-free ramen noodles, as needed (optional)

In a medium bowl, whisk together the coconut aminos, vinegar, honey, and molasses. Set the bowl aside.

Melt 2 tablespoons (30 g) of the ghee in a large skillet over medium-high heat. While the skillet heats, toss the chicken with the oil in a large bowl, and then coat the chicken with the potato starch, ginger, and sea salt until each piece of chicken is coated well.

Put the chicken into the hot skillet and cook it for 3 to 4 minutes, stirring occasionally, until the chicken is golden brown and crispy. Set the chicken aside and wipe any crumbs out of the skillet.

Set the skillet over medium heat and add the remaining 3 tablespoons (45 g) of ghee. After the ghee has melted, add the onion, bell pepper, mushrooms, and sugar snap peas. Cook the vegetables in the skillet, stirring occasionally for 10 minutes, until the veggies are starting to caramelize and are soft. Add the garlic and cook the mixture for 1 to 2 minutes, until the garlic is fragrant.

Add the crispy chicken and the coconut aminos sauce to the skillet, stirring to combine. Cook the stir-fry for about 2 minutes, until the sauce thickens from the starch on the chicken. You can add a splash of water or bone broth if you want a saucier stir-fry. Season the stir-fry with sea salt and black pepper, if desired.

Serve the stir-fry as is or over the rice or ramen noodles (if using). This stir-fry will last for up to 3 days in the refrigerator.

Note
- You can use leftover chicken from Prep-Day Whole Chicken Two Ways recipe (page 164) or use boneless, skinless breasts or thighs if you don't have cooked chicken. Coat the chicken the same way as the cooked chicken, and cook it until the chicken is cooked completely.

Yummiest Spaghetti with Veggie Monster Mini Meatballs

(dairy-free option, gluten-free, nut-free, soy-free)

Pack a pile of mineral-rich veggies into their very favorite package: spaghetti and meatballs! This hearty spaghetti meal with amazing flavors will keep them focused for a full afternoon of school and after-school activities.

Makes 15 (1-cup [200-g]) servings (including pasta; older children and teens will eat closer to 2 cups [400 g])

Monster Mini Meatballs
1 lb (450 g) ground beef

1 large egg

3 tbsp (45 ml) cream or coconut milk

¼ cup (40 g) tapioca starch

1 tbsp (9 g) onion powder

2 tsp (6 g) garlic powder

1 tsp dried oregano

1 tsp sea salt

¼ tsp black pepper

1 cup (30 g) baby spinach, finely chopped

Veggie Sauce and Spaghetti
1 lb (450 g) uncooked gluten-free pasta of choice (see Note)

3 tbsp (45 ml) olive oil

1 medium onion, diced

1 medium carrot, peeled and diced

½ medium zucchini, diced

4 oz (112 g) white button mushrooms, thinly sliced

Sea salt, as needed

3 cloves garlic, minced

1 (24-oz [720-ml]) jar spaghetti sauce of choice

Preheat the oven to 375°F (191°C). Line a large baking sheet with a silicone baking mat or unbleached parchment paper.

To make the monster mini meatballs, mix together the beef, egg, cream, tapioca starch, onion powder, garlic powder, oregano, sea salt, black pepper, and baby spinach in a small bowl. Roll 1-inch (2.5-cm) meatballs with the beef mixture, arranging them in rows on the prepared baking sheet. Bake the mini meatballs for 20 minutes, until they are golden brown on top.

While the mini meatballs bake, make the veggie sauce and spaghetti. Bring a large pot of water to a boil over high heat. Add the pasta and boil it for about 6 minutes, until it is al dente.

Meanwhile, heat the oil in a large pot over medium-high heat. Add the onion, carrot, zucchini, mushrooms, and a big pinch of sea salt. Cook the vegetables for 10 to 15 minutes, stirring occasionally, until the veggies are very soft and caramelized. (The longer the mixture cooks, the more flavor it will have.)

Add the garlic and spaghetti sauce and bring the sauce to a simmer. Cook it for 5 to 10 minutes.

Add the mini meatballs to the sauce and serve the meatballs and sauce over the cooked spaghetti.

Note
- We like the Jovial or Tinkyáda® brands of gluten-free rice spaghetti.

Back-to-School Fall Harvest Soup

(dairy-free option, egg-free, gluten-free, nut-free, soy-free)

When the weather turns cooler and school is back in session, warm the kids up after a chilly recess with this smooth sweet and savory soup! Squash is loaded with vitamins and minerals that busy, growing children need—and it also happens to have a kid-friendly sweet taste. They'll slurp this soup down from their thermos with a straw or a spoon and be ready for a full and focused afternoon of classes.

Makes 12 cups (2.9 L) soup

1 small butternut squash, peeled, seeds removed, and cubed (see Note)

1 small pie pumpkin, seeds removed and cut into eighths (see Note)

2 tbsp (30 ml) olive oil

½ tsp sea salt, plus more as needed

3 tbsp (45 g) butter or ghee or 3 tbsp (45 ml) olive oil

1 medium onion, coarsely chopped

1 large carrot, peeled and coarsely chopped

1 small sweet potato, peeled or unpeeled and cubed

3 cloves garlic

2 small pears, peeled or unpeeled and cubed

4 cups (960 ml) bone broth (page 165)

½ cup (120 ml) full-fat coconut milk or raw milk

1 tsp coconut sugar, raw honey, or pure maple syrup (optional)

Black pepper, as needed

Preheat the oven to 425°F (218°C).

On a large baking sheet, toss the butternut squash and pumpkin with the oil and sea salt. Roast the squash and pumpkin for 30 minutes, until they are fork tender.

Meanwhile, melt the butter in a large soup pot over medium heat. Add the onion, carrot, sweet potato, and a large pinch of sea salt. Cook the vegetables for 10 minutes, until the veggies are soft and slightly caramelized. Add the garlic and pears and cook the mixture for 3 to 5 minutes.

When the squash and pumpkin are done roasting and are cool enough to handle, use a knife to slice the skin away from the pumpkin. Discard the skin.

Add the broth, milk, and butternut squash and pumpkin to the soup pot. Bring the soup to a simmer. Turn the heat off and puree the soup using an immersion blender. (Alternatively, you can blend the soup in a countertop blender, working in batches if necessary.) Stir in the sugar (if using), sea salt, and black pepper.

This soup will last for 5 days in the refrigerator. To freeze the soup, let it cool to room temperature, and then store it in freezer-safe containers in the portion sizes that you want.

Note

- You could use your Instant Pot® pressure cooker to cook the squash and pumpkin if you are short on time; however, I love the flavor that roasting lends the vegetables, and by the time the Instant Pot® comes to pressure, the cooking time is almost the same as the 30 minutes of roasting time.

Easy-Prep Creamy Tuscan Bean Soup

(dairy-free option, egg-free, gluten-free, nut-free, soy-free)

They'll be warmed to the bone on those cold winter days with this satisfying, savory bean soup. Easy enough to prep for a weekday dinner, it packs up quickly for leftovers the next day, making it a reliable menu item on your weekly or monthly meal plan.

Makes 8 cups (1.9 L) soup

3 tbsp (45 g) butter plus 1 tbsp (15 g) bacon grease or 4 tbsp (60 ml) olive oil

1 large onion, diced

2 large or 3 medium carrots, peeled and diced

3 medium ribs celery, diced

Sea salt, as needed

4 to 5 cloves garlic, minced

⅛ to ¼ tsp red pepper flakes

½ cup (120 ml) white wine (or more bone broth)

4 cups (960 ml) bone broth (page 165)

½ tsp dried thyme

1 large or 2 small dried bay leaves

3 cups (540 g) canned or home-cooked navy beans (page 163), drained and rinsed

½ cup (120 ml) full-fat coconut milk, raw milk, or cream

1 to 2 cups (30 to 60 g) baby spinach or baby kale, finely chopped

Black pepper, as needed

Shredded Parmesan cheese, as needed (optional)

Melt the butter and bacon grease in a large soup pot over medium-high heat. Add the onion, carrots, celery, and a big pinch of sea salt. Stir to combine the vegetables and cook them for 10 minutes, stirring occasionally, until the veggies are soft and caramelized.

Stir in the garlic and red pepper flakes. Cook the mixture until it is fragrant, about 30 seconds. Add the wine. Bring the wine to a simmer, deglazing the pan, and let the wine simmer for 2 minutes.

Add the broth, thyme, bay leaf, and navy beans. Increase the heat to high and bring the soup to a simmer. Reduce the heat to medium and bring the soup to a low simmer, then put a lid on the pot. Simmer the soup for 10 to 15 minutes.

Turn the heat off and remove the bay leaf. Transfer 2 to 3 cups (480 to 720 ml) of the soup to a large heatproof bowl and puree it with an immersion blender. (Alternatively, you can puree the soup with a countertop blender, working in batches if necessary.) Return the pureed soup back to the soup pot. Turn on the heat to medium-high. Stir in the milk and baby spinach and simmer the soup for 1 minute to wilt the spinach. Season the soup with sea salt and black pepper to taste. Garnish the soup with the Parmesan cheese (if using).

This soup will last for up to 5 days in the refrigerator, or you can freeze the soup in freezer-safe containers for up to 3 months.

Notes

- Crispy bacon or ham is a great addition to this soup if you have it on hand.
- You can puree the entire soup and add a bit more bone broth or cream if your kids eat soup better that way.

Healthy Alphabet Soup Copycat

(dairy-free option, egg-free, gluten-free, nut-free, soy-free)

Enjoy the nostalgic red can of alphabet soup that you grew up on (and that continues to be a kid favorite) with this delicious version made with real ingredients, zero preservatives, nourishing bone broth, and super fun pasta letters. This soup is a tasty way to get some veggies into your kids' lunchbox—they will happily slurp this warm veggie soup out of their thermoses!

Makes 12 cups (2.9 L) soup

3 tbsp (45 g) butter or ghee or 3 tbsp (45 ml) olive or avocado oil

1 medium onion, diced

1 large carrot, peeled and diced

2 cups (270 g) frozen 1-inch (2.5-cm) green bean pieces

1 medium russet or yellow potato, peeled or unpeeled and diced

Sea salt, as needed

4 cloves garlic, minced

2 tbsp (34 g) tomato paste

1 cup (165 g) organic frozen corn

1 (15-oz [450-ml]) can tomato sauce

1 cup (30 g) baby spinach or baby kale, finely chopped

8 cups (1.9 L) bone broth (page 165)

1½ to 2 cups (173 to 230 g) uncooked gluten-free alphabet pasta (such as Banza brand) or small pasta of choice (such as shells or elbows)

Black pepper, as needed

Melt the butter in a large soup pot over medium-high heat. Add the onion, carrot, green beans, potato, and a big pinch of sea salt. Cook the vegetables for about 7 minutes, until the veggies soften.

Add the garlic and tomato paste, stir to combine, and cook the mixture for 1 minute.

Add the corn, tomato sauce, baby spinach, and broth and bring the soup to a simmer. Add the pasta and simmer, stirring occasionally, until the pasta is cooked to your liking, 5 to 7 minutes (depending on the brand of pasta). Season the soup with sea salt and black pepper to taste.

Note

- This soup does not freeze well with the pasta, but you can make the soup all the way to the point of putting the pasta in, and leave it out in order to freeze the soup. When you're ready to finish making the soup, you can bring the soup to a simmer and add the pasta.

Nuggets, Dippers, and Bites

I've always said, "Make anything nugget-, mini-, bite-, or dipper-size, and kids will eat it!"

When we make food "kid-sized," something magical happens. The food doesn't feel so overwhelming to children when it is small—and, let's be honest, it's fun to dip and eat little bites with our hands! The food industry has learned the magic of bite-size and dipper-shaped food, at the expense of putting a load of preservatives, sugar, salt, and food dyes into our growing children. I say there has to be a better way! Our children are worth more than cheap, processed ingredients. And their rapidly growing bodies deserve fuel that will spark the creativity and drive they were designed to exhibit during these important years, when their brains are absorbing and learning about everything around them.

It really is possible to make exciting, kid-favorite bites, like classic crispy chicken nuggets (page 78) and meatballs just the right size for little hands (page 82). In this chapter, I've made crispy fish sticks in healthy, brain-nourishing fat (page 81); created a fun, lunchbox-friendly twist on canned sloppy joes (page 85); and even developed a healthier prep for mini carnival-style corn dogs (page 87). With busy parents in mind, these little bites, nuggets, and dippers are realistic in prep time, freezable, and, of course, kid-approved in taste!

How to Pack These Nuggets, Dippers, and Bites for a Balanced Lunchbox

All of the recipes in this chapter are great sources of protein and fat. With the veggie nuggets (page 95) as the exception, all you'll need to balance these recipes in a lunchbox is a side of veggies and fruit. The veggie nuggets would benefit from an extra side of protein and fat, perhaps in the form of yogurt or cheese, trail mix (try my recipe on page 125), rolled-up deli meat or jerky, or beans. All of the recipes in this section freeze well! You can cook them on a prep day or make them for dinner, then pack up the leftovers into freezer-safe bags for storage.

Five-Ingredient Fast-Prep Chicken Nuggets

(dairy-free, gluten-free, nut-free, soy-free)

Is it really this simple to make chicken nuggets? My goal in developing this recipe was to get you away from boxed or bagged frozen nuggets with mile-long lists of ingredients, and I can promise these crispy nuggets will not disappoint. With a short ingredient list and a five-minute prep, you'll never know these nuggets were baked instead of fried with their crispy exterior, juicy interior, and amazing flavor!

Makes about 28 (1-inch [2.5-cm]) chicken nuggets

1 cup (55 g) gluten-free panko bread crumbs (such as Ian's or Jeff Nathan Creations brands)

1 tsp sea salt

1 large egg

1 lb (450 g) boneless, skinless chicken breasts

Avocado or olive oil spray, as needed

Preheat the oven to 425°F (218°C). Line a large baking sheet with a silicone baking mat or unbleached parchment paper.

Put the bread crumbs and sea salt in a gallon zip-top bag and shake to combine them. In a small bowl, whisk the egg. Set the bread crumbs and egg aside.

Lightly pat the chicken dry and cut it into 1-inch (2.5-cm) pieces. Transfer the chicken in the bowl with the egg and stir to combine, so that every piece of chicken is coated in egg.

Put the coated chicken pieces into the bag of bread crumbs. Close the bag and shake it to coat the chicken in the crumbs. Place the breaded chicken nuggets on the prepared baking sheet.

Spray the nuggets with the oil spray. Bake them for 20 minutes, until they are golden brown on top. Place the cooked nuggets on a wire rack to cool.

Chicken nuggets will last 3 days in the refrigerator. To freeze the cooked chicken nuggets, cool them completely and freeze them in a freezer-safe bag for up to 3 months. You can put the chicken nuggets into lunchboxes frozen and they will thaw by lunchtime.

Serve the nuggets with your kids' favorite dipping sauce, such as ketchup, honey mustard, or Easy Homemade Ranch (page 156).

Notes

- If your kids like honey mustard to dip, simply stir up a 2:1 ratio of mustard to raw honey for an easy, fun dipping sauce!
- This recipe doubles perfectly—just use two baking sheets. Doubling will help with having enough leftovers from dinner to put into lunchboxes—or you will be able to have a large stash for your freezer!

Kid-Favorite Crispy Fish Stick Dippers

(dairy-free, gluten-free, nut-free, soy-free)

Fish sticks are a crispy and delicious way to get protein into lunchboxes.
Not only are these fish sticks satisfying with their savory fried flavor, they are also
packed with brain-boosting power and energy from the omega-3 fatty acids in the fish
and healthy medium-chain fatty acids (like caprylic acid and lauric acid) from
being cooked in the coconut oil!

Makes 18 to 20 fish stick dippers or about 30 dipper bites

1 large egg

1 cup (55 g) gluten-free panko bread crumbs (such as Ian's or Jeff Nathan Creations brands)

½ tsp smoked paprika

1 tsp garlic powder

1 tsp sea salt

¼ tsp black pepper

¼ to ⅓ cup (60 to 80 g) coconut oil or ghee (or a combination of both)

4 (4- to 6-oz [112- to 170-g]) whitefish fillets (mahi-mahi or cod work best)

Dipping sauce of choice, as needed (see Note)

In a small bowl, whisk the egg. Set the bowl aside.

In a gallon zip-top bag, combine the bread crumbs, smoked paprika, garlic powder, sea salt, and black pepper. Shake the bag to combine the ingredients. Set the bag aside.

Melt the oil in a medium skillet over medium-high heat.

While the oil is melting, pat the fish fillets dry. Cut them into 2-inch (5-cm) fish sticks or 1-inch (2.5-cm) bites. If using cod, be gentle when handling as it is delicate. Put the fish sticks into the bowl with the whisked egg, and stir to combine so that every piece of fish is coated in egg.

Put the coated fish sticks into the bag with the seasoned bread crumbs, close the bag, and shake it gently to completely coat the fish in the bread crumbs.

Put the breaded fish sticks into the hot oil in the skillet, being careful not to overcrowd the skillet. (Work in batches if necessary to avoid overcrowding the skillet.) Cook the fish sticks until the outside of the fish crisps up and is a deep golden brown on each side, about 2 minutes for sticks and about 1 minute for bites. (If you made your fish sticks very thick or larger, cook them longer to ensure the middle of the fish is cooked through.)

Place the cooked fish sticks on a wire rack while you cook another batch. Continue this process until all the fish sticks are cooked.

Cooked fish sticks keep in the refrigerator for 3 days, or they can be frozen in freezer-safe bags for up to 3 months.

Pack your fish stick dippers with a condiment container filled with your child's preferred dipping sauce, such as ketchup or tartar sauce.

Note

- If your kids love tartar sauce, mix full-fat sour cream or mayo with chopped pickles and a dash of pickle juice. Season with salt, black pepper, and raw honey to your kids' taste and—voilà!—tartar sauce.

Easy-Prep Sheet Pan Meatballs

(dairy-free, gluten-free, nut-free, soy-free)

Every busy family needs a staple meatball recipe! This go-to sheet pan meatball recipe will be on your meal plan week after week, thanks to its kid-approved taste and mom-approved healthy ingredients—not to mention a prep time that will make whomever does the cooking in your house jump for joy! You can make the meatballs for dinner with gravy, tossed with buttered pasta, or on a bed of roasted veggies, and then use the leftover meatballs with condiment containers of marinara sauce, ketchup, or Easy Homemade Ranch (page 156) for the lunchbox.

Makes 20 to 25 meatballs

1 lb (450 g) ground beef

1 large egg

¼ cup (38 g) white rice flour

3 tbsp (45 ml) full-fat coconut milk, cream, or whole milk

1 tbsp (12 g) nutritional yeast or ¼ cup (45 g) grated Parmesan cheese

1 tbsp (9 g) onion powder

2 tsp (6 g) garlic powder

2 tsp (6 g) Italian seasoning

1 tsp sea salt

¼ tsp black pepper

Preheat the oven to 375°F (191°C). Line a large baking sheet with a silicone baking mat or unbleached parchment paper.

In a small bowl, mix together the beef, egg, flour, milk, nutritional yeast, onion powder, garlic powder, Italian seasoning, sea salt, and black pepper using your hands or a rubber spatula. Use the beef mixture to make 1- to 2-inch (2.5- to 5-cm) meatballs and place them on the prepared baking sheet.

Bake 1-inch (2.5-cm) meatballs for 20 minutes, and 2-inch (5-cm) meatballs for 25 minutes. When they are done, the meatballs will be lightly browned on top.

The meatballs will last for 3 days in the refrigerator. To freeze the meatballs, let them cool completely and then store them in a freezer-safe bag for up to 3 months. You can pull the meatballs from the freezer and put them straight into the lunchbox and they will thaw by lunchtime.

Notes

- You can also add kale or spinach to the mixture without affecting the taste. Simply put ¼ to ½ cup (8 to 15 g) of finely chopped baby spinach or baby kale to the meat mixture.

- Change up the flavor of the meatballs if you like. Swap the Italian seasoning for curry powder, and pack the curry meatballs with a peanut dipping sauce. Make them Mexican-flavored with taco seasoning and pack along salsa for dipping.

Lunchbox-Friendly, Real-Food Sloppy Joe Bites

(dairy-free option, egg-free, gluten-free, nut-free, soy-free)

I took the sloppy out of the sloppy joes for these little mess-free sloppy joe bites! They supply all of the deliciousness of that favorite can of Manwich® sauce from your childhood with a copycat flavor made with only clean, real-food ingredients. Put a smile on their faces when they open their lunchboxes to find their beloved sloppy joe dinner remade into a bite-size, exciting lunch.

Makes 26 sloppy joe bites plus 2½ cups (600 g) leftover sloppy joe filling (for sloppy joes on buns or as a topping for baked potatoes)

Sloppy Joes

1 tbsp (15 g) butter or ghee or 1 tbsp (15 ml) olive or avocado oil

2 lbs (900 g) ground beef

1 tsp sea salt, divided

1 small onion, diced

1 medium red or orange bell pepper, diced

4 cloves garlic, minced

2 tsp (6 g) chili powder

2 tsp (6 g) smoked paprika

2 tbsp (34 g) tomato paste

2 tbsp (30 g) yellow mustard

3 tbsp (45 ml) pure maple syrup

1 tsp molasses

1 (15-oz [450-ml]) can tomato sauce

1 cup (240 ml) bone broth (page 165) or water

To make the sloppy joes, melt the butter in a large skillet over medium-high heat. Add the beef and ½ teaspoon of the sea salt. Cook the beef for 5 to 7 minutes, until it has browned. Remove the browned beef from the skillet and set it aside, reserving about 3 tablespoons (45 ml) of the cooking fat in the skillet.

Set the skillet over medium heat. Add the onion, bell pepper, and the remaining ½ teaspoon of sea salt. Cook the veggies for 7 minutes, until they are soft. Add the garlic and cook for 1 minute.

Return the beef to the skillet, then add the chili powder, smoked paprika, tomato paste, mustard, maple syrup, molasses, tomato sauce, and broth. Bring the mixture to a simmer, using a potato masher or a stiff spoon to break up the beef into the sauce. Simmer the sloppy joe mixture for 15 minutes, until it thickens.

(continued)

Lunchbox-Friendly, Real-Food Sloppy Joe Bites (cont.)

Mini Biscuit Cups

Avocado or olive oil spray, as needed

2 cups (244 g) Namaste Perfect Flour Blend or 2 cups (280 g) Otto's brand cassava flour (see Notes)

1¼ cups (300 ml) full-fat coconut milk or milk (or 1¾ cups [420 ml] if you are using cassava flour)

2 tbsp (30 ml) apple cider vinegar

2 tsp (8 g) aluminum-free baking powder

1 tsp sea salt

2 tsp (10 ml) raw honey

While the sloppy joe mixture simmers, make the mini biscuit cups. Preheat the oven to 400°F (204°C). Spray a mini muffin pan with the oil spray.

In a medium bowl, combine the flour, milk, vinegar, baking powder, sea salt, and honey. Stir to create a ball of dough.

Oil your hands lightly and pinch off some dough. Roll it into a 1-inch (2.5-cm) ball, and place the ball of dough into one of the mini muffin pan cups. Gently use your thumb to press the dough down to the bottom and up the sides of the muffin cup. The dough should come up over the edge a bit to hold 1 tablespoon (15 g) of sloppy joe filling. Continue filling the muffin cups with the dough.

Scoop 1 tablespoon (15 g) of the sloppy joe mixture into each of the biscuit dough cups. Bake the sloppy joe bites for 15 to 18 minutes, until the biscuits are set.

The sloppy joe bites will last for 3 days in the refrigerator. To freeze the sloppy joe bites, cool them completely and store them in freezer-safe bags in the freezer for up to 3 months. You can put them into the lunchbox frozen and they will thaw by lunchtime.

Notes

- Use your sloppy joe bites for lunchboxes, and then use the leftover 2½ cups (600 g) of sloppy joe mixture for your sloppy joe dinner night on traditional buns (or over baked potatoes or sweet potatoes if you are grain-free). Alternatively, you can double the biscuit recipe and make more sloppy joe bites.

- I have made these grain-free using Otto's brand cassava flour. Use the same amount of everything in the biscuit recipe, except increase the coconut milk to 1¾ cups (420 ml). Results may differ if you use a different brand of gluten-free flour or cassava flour.

- To make this recipe more budget-friendly, swap 1 pound (450 g) of the beef for cooked pinto or red beans. See page 163 for my Instant Pot® cooking method. Alternatively, you can use drained and rinsed canned beans.

Carnival Copycat Corn Dogs

(dairy-free, gluten-free, nut-free, soy-free)

These sweet bites remind me of summertime in my little beach town, where the coolest place to get a quick lunch is this tiny corn dog stand by the channel where the boats come in. Now you can bring that nostalgic flavor to the kids' lunchboxes in a healthier way using healthy cooking fat and better ingredients!

Makes 12 mini corn dogs

4 large or 6 regular hot dogs (see Notes)

¾ cup (92 g) gluten-free flour blend (such as Namaste Perfect Flour Blend), divided

¾ cup (180 g) coconut oil (see Notes)

½ cup (85 g) coarsely or finely ground cornmeal

2 tsp (8 g) aluminum-free baking powder

¼ tsp sea salt

1 tsp raw honey

1 large egg

¾ cup (180 ml) full-fat coconut milk or whole milk

If you are using large hot dogs, cut them into thirds. If you are using regular hot dogs, cut them in half. Skewer the hot dogs with halved Popsicle sticks or small, blunt skewers. Put ¼ cup (31 g) of the flour on a small plate. Pat the hot dogs dry with a paper towel, and roll the skewered hot dogs in the flour just until they are dusted with flour—you can roll them, then tap off the excess if needed. This helps the batter stick.

Melt the oil in a small saucepan over medium heat.

While the oil melts, use a spoon to mix the cornmeal, remaining ½ cup (61 g) of flour, baking powder, sea salt, honey, egg, and milk in a 2-cup (480-ml) liquid measuring cup. (A Mason jar would work too—you need a container deep enough to make dipping the hot dogs easy.)

Dip a hot dog into the corn dog batter, shake off the excess, and then gently lower it into the hot oil. Fry it for about 10 seconds, then turn it around to ensure even cooking. Fry the corn dog for about 1 minute, until all sides are a deep, dark golden brown and cooked through.

(continued)

Once the corn dog is cooked, place it on a wire rack or paper towel to cool, and move on to the next corn dog. Continue this process until all the corn dogs are cooked.

To freeze the corn dogs, let them cool completely, and then store them in a freezer-safe bag for up to 3 months. You can pull the corn dogs from the freezer and place them right in the lunchbox in the morning, and they will be thawed by lunchtime.

Notes

- I use the Teton Waters Ranch brand grass-fed beef hot dogs. Applegate Organics® brand hot dogs work great too. Or if you have a local farmer that makes grass-fed hot dogs, that is even better.

- Grass-fed tallow or lard or avocado oil will work instead of coconut oil, as they have a higher smoke point, making them safe for high-heat cooking.

- You will have about ½ cup (120 ml) of corn dog batter left after making the corn dogs. It is harder to dip them when the batter is made in a smaller amount. You can freeze this batter and add it to the batter the next time you make the corn dogs or make even smaller corn dogs with bite-size hot dogs stirred up in the remaining batter. I have done this and, while messy for your fingers, it works and they turn out really cute!

Fun and Fast Grilled Cheese Dunkers

(egg-free, gluten-free, nut-free, soy-free)

Gooey Manchego cheese meets sweet apple and salty bacon! Let them feel like they are in a fun sandwich shop with these crispy grilled cheese dunkers—my older girls even proclaimed they tasted just like a sandwich shop grilled cheese, and you can't beat a thermos of Creamy Tomato Bisque (page 57) to dunk them in.

Makes 2 full sandwiches, cut into 4 to 5 dunkers (depending on the size of the bread slices)

2 tbsp (30 g) softened butter

4 slices gluten-free bread of choice

½ to 1 cup (40 to 80 g) shredded Manchego cheese (or more, depending on the size of the bread)

½ small sweet or tart apple, thinly sliced

2 strips bacon, cooked until crispy (or more, depending on the size of the bread)

Preheat a panini maker according to the manufacturer's instructions while you assemble the sandwiches. (Alternatively, you can use a griddle, flattop grill, or a skillet to toast your grilled cheese.)

Butter one side of each piece of bread. Flip the bread over so that the buttered side is facing down and divide the Manchego cheese, apple slices, and bacon between 2 of the pieces of bread. (You may want to end with a little cheese on top so it sticks to the other slice of bread.) Top the sandwich filling with the second piece of bread with the buttered side facing outward.

Grill the sandwiches on the panini maker for 1 to 2 minutes, until they are golden brown. Use a long, sharp knife to cut the sandwiches into strips to create handheld dunkers.

Grilled cheese dunkers will last for up to 3 days in the refrigerator.

Notes

- You can swap the cheese for whatever you have on hand or love the best. Watch ingredients and go for blocks of real cheese versus processed squares or bagged shredded cheese to avoid hidden ingredients. I love the creaminess of Manchego, and in my family—with two of us on the dairy-sensitive side—we tolerate sheep's milk easier than cow's milk. Goat's milk cheeses work well for these and is my oldest child's favorite way to eat a grilled cheese.

- The flatbreads from the Pizza Lunchables® Copycat (page 34) work well on the panini maker for this recipe too!

- The pesto from my "Charcuterie Board" Lunchbox (page 49) makes a pretty spread on the inside of this sandwich.

Nourishing Mini Quiche Bites

(dairy-free, gluten-free, nut-free, soy-free)

Make the most of your weekend brunch: Plan these little quiches into your Saturday morning, and pack the leftovers away for the easiest Tuesday lunchbox you've ever made. These mini egg muffins are definitely little-hands approved!

Makes 48 mini quiches

Avocado oil spray

12 large eggs

¼ cup (28 g) coconut flour

¼ cup (60 ml) olive oil

¼ cup (60 ml) water

1 tsp flaxseed meal

1 tbsp (9 g) onion powder

1 tsp garlic powder

1½ tsp (8 g) sea salt

½ cup (45 g) finely chopped broccoli

½ cup (67 g) finely chopped sweet potato

Preheat the oven to 350°F (177°C). Line a 48-cup mini muffin pan with mini silicone muffin cup liners or spray the pan with the oil spray.

In a medium mixing bowl, whisk together the eggs, flour, oil, water, flaxseed meal, onion powder, garlic powder, and sea salt. Stir in the broccoli and sweet potato.

Scoop the egg mixture into the prepared muffin pan, filling each cup almost to the top. (I use a ¼-cup [60-g] measuring cup to scoop the egg mixture, and 1 mini muffin cup is about half of that.)

Bake the mini quiches for 17 minutes, until they spring back when touched.

Mini quiches will last for 3 days in the refrigerator. To freeze the mini quiches, let them cool completely before putting them into a freezer-safe bag and freezing them flat for up to 3 months.

Notes

- If you do not have a mini muffin pan, you can use a regular muffin pan and regular-sized silicone muffin cup liners or unbleached parchment paper liners to bake the quiches. Increase the baking time to 25 minutes for the larger quiches.

- You can add up to ½ cup (60 g) of shredded cow's cheese or goat cheese to the egg mixture if you tolerate them. If you add the cheese, reduce the sea salt to 1 teaspoon since the cheese has a salty bite.

- Use whatever veggies are in season: asparagus and leeks in the spring, bell peppers and broccoli in the summer, mushrooms and spinach in the fall, and kale and sweet potatoes in the winter!

The Best Busy Kid-Approved Veggie Nuggets

(dairy-free, gluten-free, nut-free, soy-free)

Even broccoli will be happily gobbled up when you make it nugget-size!
These kid-sized vegetable nuggets are packed with three different vegetables loaded
with minerals to keep your busy scholars functioning to their best ability.
With zero preservatives and simpler ingredients, you can save money on overpriced
store-bought veggie tots and make your own healthier version.

Makes 28 veggie nuggets

Avocado or olive oil spray, as needed

3 cups (270 g) coarsely chopped broccoli florets

2 cups (300 g) shredded sweet potato

1 cup (50 g) shredded carrot

1 clove garlic, cut in half

⅓ cup (57 g) potato flour (do not use potato starch)

¼ cup (28 g) coconut flour

2 large eggs

2 tsp (6 g) onion powder

1 tbsp (12 g) nutritional yeast (optional)

1 tsp sea salt

¼ tsp black pepper

Dip of choice

Preheat the oven to 425°F (218°C). Put a baking rack on a large baking sheet, and spray the rack with the oil spray (or use a paper towel to rub the baking rack with avocado oil).

In a food processor, combine the broccoli, sweet potato, carrot, garlic, potato flour, coconut flour, eggs, onion powder, nutritional yeast (if using), sea salt, and black pepper. Pulse the mixture a few times to break up the ingredients, and then process to fully combine them. You will need to scrape the edges down a couple times at first, and the mixture will look dry in the beginning, but do not add more liquid. Keep processing and the mixture will pull together almost like a dough. The vegetable pieces should be nice and small, and the mixture should be thick and easy to roll up in your hands.

Scoop out about 1 tablespoon (15 g) of the veggie nugget mixture, gently roll it into a ball, and then shape it however you want the nugget to look, flattening the nugget until it is about ½ inch (13 mm) thick. Place the veggie nugget onto the baking rack, and continue making the rest of the nuggets, lining them up on the baking rack.

Bake the veggie nuggets for 30 minutes, until they are light golden brown on top. Let the nuggets cool for 5 minutes before transferring them to a baking rack or serving immediately.

Veggie nuggets will last for up to 5 days in the refrigerator. To freeze the veggie nuggets, cool them completely and store them in a freezer-safe bag in the freezer for up to 3 months. You can put them into lunchboxes directly from the freezer and they will thaw by lunchtime.

Pack the veggie nuggets with a condiment container of dip, such as ketchup, honey mustard, Super Smooth Kid-Favorite Hummus (page 158), or Easy Homemade Ranch (page 156).

Colorful Kid-Approved Salads

Get their veggies in with exciting, kid-inspired salad dressings, colorful presentations, and delicious, filling ingredients!

It's time to give kids a little more credit: When it comes to eating their vegetables, they can be known for more than just that bottle of ranch dressing. Kids' palates are capable of so much more, and their growing bodies deserve better fuel. Fun salad dressings and delicious ingredients take the fight out of eating their veggies, and when salads and dressings are made with healthy, brain-boosting fats, they make a nourishing addition to the lunchbox.

If salads haven't been your child's top choice for lunch-packing, get ready to make a change! With fun, fruity dressings like the Sweet Orange Vinaigrette in the Superhero Quinoa Salad (page 107), and the Fruity Poppy Seed Dressing in the Colorful Rainbow Chicken Salad (page 103), your kids will be requesting salads weekly. And the easy-to-eat pasta salads—such as the Kid-Approved Broccoli Pesto Pasta Salad (page 115) and the Fast-Prep, Brain-Boosting Bow Tie Pasta Salad (page 98)—are perfect ways to encourage your younger children to eat veggies. Try introducing your little ones to the new salads at dinner first so that the meal becomes a familiar food. Before you know it, you can add these exciting new salads to your lunchbox rotation!

How to Pack These Colorful Kid-Approved Salads for a Balanced Lunchbox

With the exception of the Real-Food Dole® Fruit Cup Copycat (page 111), all of the salads in this section are a great source of fat and definitely help your kids get their veggies in! If the salad doesn't represent a source of protein, such as the pasta salads and the veggie noodle salad, add some hard-boiled eggs, yogurt, Fast-Prep Healthy Trail Mix (page 125), or meat as lunchbox sides. If the salad is a good meal, with a balance of protein, fat, and carbs—such as the Colorful Rainbow Chicken Salad with Fruity Poppy Seed Dressing (page 103)—then you can just add some simple sides like an apple or other in-season fruit and maybe some crunchy sides like pretzels or seeds and nuts. The fruit salad on page 111 is a good fruit addition to any lunchbox. But remember that you'll want to have protein and fat represented in other foods for a balanced lunchbox.

Fast-Prep, Brain-Boosting Bow Tie Pasta Salad

(dairy-free option, egg-free, gluten-free, nut-free, soy-free)

As a summer picnic staple, pasta salad is destined for lunch-packing! This colorful chilled pasta salad is dressed with brain-nourishing olive oil and tastes great cold. With kid-favorite veggies like peas and appealing pasta shapes, this dish makes a fun and nourishing lunchbox salad.

Makes 10 (1-cup [200-g]) servings (smaller children will eat approximately ½ cup [100 g] and adults may eat more than 1 cup [200 g])

¾ cup (180 ml) plus 2 tbsp (30 ml) olive oil, divided

2 tbsp (30 ml) white wine vinegar or distilled white vinegar

1 tsp raw honey

1½ tsp (8 g) sea salt

1 tsp dried oregano

1 tsp dried parsley

½ tsp garlic powder

½ tsp onion powder

¼ tsp black pepper

Pinch of dried thyme

1 (1-lb [450-g]) bag uncooked gluten-free pasta of choice (such as Jovial brand gluten-free)

1 to 2 cups (138 to 276 g) diced summer sausage or kielbasa

1 cup (175 g) quartered cherry tomatoes

1 cup (50 g) finely chopped green onions

1 cup (175 g) diced bell peppers

1 cup (150 g) frozen peas (see Note)

½ cup (90 g) grated Parmesan cheese, raw cheese, or goat cheese (optional)

Fill a large pot with water and set it over high heat to come to a boil while you get the rest of the ingredients ready.

In a large bowl, whisk together ¾ cup (180 ml) of the oil, vinegar, honey, sea salt, oregano, parsley, garlic powder, onion powder, black pepper, and thyme.

When the water comes to a boil, add the remaining 2 tablespoons (30 ml) of oil to the water. Add the pasta to the boiling water, and cook it until it is al dente (the pasta needs to have "bite," because it will soak in the dressing).

Drain the cooked pasta and immediately add it to the dressing in the large bowl. Stir the pasta to coat it evenly with the dressing. Fold in the summer sausage, tomatoes, green onions, bell peppers, and peas.

Chill the pasta for at least 2 hours if you want to serve it cold, stirring the Parmesan cheese (if using) into the pasta salad once it is chilled. (This salad is delicious warm too. If you choose to serve it warm, stir in the Parmesan cheese immediately so it can melt.)

This pasta salad lasts for up to 3 days in the refrigerator.

Note

- Change up the veggies! Another favorite in my house is to use chopped fresh green beans in place of the peas—you can blanch them quickly or use them raw. I have also used chopped baby spinach, which wilts perfectly when mixed with the hot pasta. A frozen pea and carrot mix is nice too!

Taco Tuesday Fajita Salad

(dairy-free option, egg-free, gluten-free, nut-free, soy-free)

Everybody—even kids—needs something to look forward to on an otherwise mundane Tuesday! Pack Taco Tuesday with flavor and fun colors with this pretty fajita salad. The creamy, Mexican-inspired dressing is full of friendly fat for a satisfied and focused afternoon.

Makes 2 cups (480 ml) dressing

Fajita Seasoning

4 tbsp (36 g) chili powder

2 tbsp (18 g) ground cumin

2 tbsp (18 g) sweet paprika

1 tbsp (12 g) coconut sugar

1 tbsp (15 g) sea salt

2 tsp (6 g) garlic powder

2 tsp (6 g) onion powder

¼ to ½ tsp cayenne pepper

Fajita Salad Dressing

¾ cup (180 ml) salsa

½ medium avocado

⅓ cup (40 g) full-fat sour cream or coconut yogurt (see Notes)

Juice of ½ small lime

1 tbsp (9 g) fajita seasoning

To make the Fajita Seasoning, whisk together the chili powder, cumin, paprika, sugar, sea salt, garlic powder, onion powder, and cayenne pepper in a medium jar. This seasoning will keep in your pantry indefinitely. It can be used to season any kind of meat or beans for fajita night anytime.

To make the Fajita Salad Dressing, combine the salsa, avocado, sour cream, lime juice, and fajita seasoning in a pint-sized (475-ml) Mason jar. Use an immersion blender to blend the ingredients until they are smooth. (Alternatively, blend the ingredients in a counter-top blender or food processor.) The Fajita Salad Dressing will keep in the fridge for 1 week.

(continued)

Fajita Chicken

1 tbsp (15 g) butter or 1 tbsp (15 ml) olive oil

2 cups (280 g) cubed or shredded cooked chicken (see Notes)

1 tbsp (9 g) Fajita Seasoning

Fajita Salad

Shredded lettuce, as needed

Fajita Chicken, as needed

Thinly sliced bell peppers (any color), as needed

Organic frozen corn, thawed, as needed

Cooked black beans (page 163), as needed

Cherry tomatoes, quartered, as needed

Shredded raw cheese or goat cheese (optional), as needed

To make the Fajita Chicken, melt the butter in a medium skillet over medium heat. Add the cooked chicken and Fajita Seasoning. Stir to combine and cook the chicken until it reaches your desired doneness.

To assemble the Fajita Salad, top the lettuce with any or all of the salad ingredients: Fajita Chicken, bell peppers, corn, black beans, tomatoes, and cheese (if using). Pack the Fajita Salad Dressing in a condiment container.

Notes

- Instead of yogurt, you can use the other half of the avocado.
- You can use the recipe for Prep-Day Whole Chicken Two Ways (page 164) on a weekly basis so that you always have chicken on hand for making recipes like this one. You could alternatively brown skinless, boneless chicken breast or thighs for this recipe if you don't have precooked chicken.

Colorful Rainbow Chicken Salad with Fruity Poppy Seed Dressing

(dairy-free option, egg-free, gluten-free, nut-free, soy-free)

The kids may never want another type of salad dressing after they taste this fun, fruit-infused veggie topper! The sky is the limit on fruit options for this salad—from strawberries to pears, you can tailor the poppy seed dressing to use whatever fruit is in season and dress up this colorful chicken salad with a rainbow of flavor.

Makes 8 oz (240 ml) dressing

Fruity Poppy Seed Dressing

1 cup (175 g) chopped fruit of choice (such as strawberries, mangoes, raspberries, oranges, pears, or clementine slices)

2 tbsp (30 g) full-fat cream cheese, full-fat yogurt, coconut yogurt, or full-fat sour cream

1 tsp red wine vinegar or balsamic vinegar

1 tsp Dijon mustard

1 tbsp (15 ml) raw honey

Pinch of sea salt, plus more as needed

¼ cup (60 ml) olive oil

1 tsp poppy seeds

To make the Fruity Poppy Seed Dressing, combine the fruit, cream cheese, vinegar, mustard, honey, and sea salt in a food processor. Process the ingredients to combine them. With the food processor running, slowly drizzle in the oil through the hole in the food processor's lid so the dressing emulsifies. Taste and season the dressing for salt. Pour the dressing into an 8-ounce (240-ml) Mason jar. Stir the poppy seeds into the dressing, and store it in the refrigerator for up to 1 week. Use a condiment container to pack the dressing for lunchboxes.

(continued)

Rainbow Chicken Salad

Chopped lettuce, as needed

Cooked cubed, shredded, or sliced chicken (see Notes), as needed

Shredded purple cabbage, as needed

Diced yellow, red, or orange bell peppers, as needed

Rainbow carrots, cut to preference, as needed (see Notes)

Sugar snap peas or frozen peas, as needed

Raw unsalted sunflower seeds, as needed

Fruity Poppy Seed Dressing, as needed

To make the Rainbow Chicken Salad, assemble the salad by topping the lettuce with the chicken, cabbage, bell peppers, carrots, sugar snap peas, and sunflower seeds. Dress the salad with the Fruity Poppy Seed Dressing according to your preference.

Notes

- The dressing recipe typically is enough to feed my whole family of five for one meal. The dressing doubles very well, so you can make more if you wish.

- The dressing works without the poppy seeds if you don't have them or the kids don't like them—they sure make the dressing fun and pretty, though!

- You can use leftover chicken from dinner using the Prep-Day Whole Chicken Two Ways recipe (page 164).

- When it comes to carrots, I like using my crinkle cutter! You can also use a star cutter. Or you can shred or dice the carrots too.

- There are so many fun, colorful toppings to choose from to change things up: cucumbers (use a star or other shape to cut them), frozen corn, cherry tomatoes, celery, and dried fruit (like goji berries, cranberries, or mangoes).

- Hard-boiled eggs swap well for the chicken, or you can leave the protein out if you plan to pack protein elsewhere in the lunchbox.

Superhero Quinoa Salad

(dairy-free, egg-free, gluten-free, nut-free, soy-free)

Their favorite superhero has nothing on this fully loaded salad bursting with protein, friendly fats, and energy-packed carbohydrates! Tossed with a tasty orange dressing and topped with crispy seeds and mandarin slices, they'll have the laser focus of a superhero for the rest of the school day.

Makes 4 (1-cup [185-g]) servings (small children will likely eat
¼ to ½ cup [46 to 93 g] per serving)

Salad

½ cup (85 g) uncooked quinoa

1 cup (240 ml) bone broth (page 165) or water

1 medium sweet potato, cut into ½-inch (13-mm) cubes

2 cups (350 g) small broccoli florets

2 tbsp (30 ml) olive oil

1 cup (165 g) canned or home-cooked chickpeas (page 163), drained and rinsed if needed

Raw pumpkin seeds or raw unsalted sunflower seeds, as needed

Mandarin oranges, peeled and separated into sections, as needed

Sea salt, as needed

Sweet Orange Vinaigrette

⅓ to ½ cup (80 to 120 ml) fresh orange juice

2 tbsp (30 ml) olive oil

1 tbsp (15 ml) pure maple syrup

1 tbsp (15 g) Dijon mustard

1 tsp apple cider vinegar

¼ tsp sea salt, or as needed

To make the salad, preheat the oven to 425°F (218°C).

Put the quinoa and broth in a medium saucepan over high heat and bring the quinoa to a boil. Reduce the heat to medium, put a lid on the saucepan, and simmer the quinoa for 15 minutes. Turn off the heat and let the saucepan sit, covered, for 5 minutes to allow the quinoa to absorb all of the liquid. Put the cooked quinoa in a medium bowl and set it aside to cool.

While the quinoa is cooking, toss together the sweet potato, broccoli, and oil on a large unlined baking sheet. Roast the veggies for 10 minutes. Add the chickpeas to the baking sheet and stir the veggies and chickpeas together. Roast the veggies and chickpeas for 15 to 20 minutes, until everything is soft and golden brown.

To make the Sweet Orange Vinaigrette, combine the orange juice, oil, maple syrup, mustard, vinegar, and sea salt in a pint-sized (475-ml) Mason jar. Use an immersion blender to blend the dressing ingredients until they are homogenous. (Alternatively, whisk together the ingredients in a small bowl if you don't have an immersion blender.)

Add the roasted veggies and chickpeas and Sweet Orange Vinaigrette to the quinoa. Toss to combine the ingredients. Season to taste with salt if needed. Set the salad in the refrigerator to cool completely. This quinoa salad lasts for up to 3 days in the refrigerator.

Just before serving, garnish the salad with the pumpkin seeds and mandarin orange slices. Leave these garnishes on the side in the lunchbox so they don't get soggy.

Note
- You can use leftover quinoa from dinner. You'll need 1 cup (185 g) of cooked quinoa.

Veggie Noodle Salad with Kid-Friendly Asian Dressing

(dairy-free, egg-free, gluten-free, nut-free option, soy-free)

Sometimes all it takes is transforming the look of a salad into something fun—like curly noodle shapes—to break a lunchbox rut! You can pick up a spiralizer just about anywhere these days, and spiralizing makes eating raw veggies much easier.

Makes ½ cup (120 ml) dressing; 8 (1-cup [240-g]) servings veggie noodle salad with 2 tbsp (30 ml) dressing (younger children will likely eat ½ cup [120 g] salad)

Kid-Friendly Asian Dressing

¼ cup (60 ml) olive oil

¼ cup (60 ml) coconut aminos

1½ tbsp (17 g) natural peanut butter, almond butter, or sunflower seed butter

1 tsp raw honey

½ tsp ground ginger

¼ tsp garlic powder

¼ tsp onion powder

Pinch of red pepper flakes (optional)

Sea salt, as needed (see Notes)

Black pepper, as needed

Veggie Noodle Salad

1 large zucchini, spiralized

2 large, thick carrots, spiralized

1 small yellow beet, spiralized

1 to 2 green onions, finely chopped (optional)

Crushed walnuts or raw unsalted sunflower seeds, as needed

To make the Kid-Friendly Asian Dressing, combine the oil, coconut aminos, peanut butter, honey, ginger, garlic powder, onion powder, red pepper flakes (if using), and salt and pepper to taste in a pint-sized (475-ml) Mason jar. Put the lid on the jar, and shake the jar vigorously to combine the dressing. Set the dressing aside. The dressing lasts for 2 weeks in the refrigerator, so it can be made ahead of time if needed.

To make the Veggie Noodle Salad, toss together the zucchini, carrots, beet, and green onions (if using) in a medium bowl. At this point, you can add the dressing and walnuts to the salad and eat the salad right away, or you can pack the dressing separately for lunchboxes so the noodles will not get soggy. Pack the walnuts on the side as well—if they are salted, they will make the veggie noodles release their water and the salad will get soggy.

Notes

- Coconut aminos are salty like soy sauce—add salt after you make the dressing, because you may not need it.

- My spiralizer can make three different sizes of "noodles." I use the thicker noodle size for this salad.

- Long, spiralized veggie noodles can be clumsy to manage at school, so if you have little ones, I recommend cutting the veggie noodles smaller for lunchboxes.

- If you have a kiddo that doesn't care for the peanut dressing, simply use his or her favorite. There are no rules to this salad! It also tastes great with my Easy Homemade Ranch (page 156).

- Ribbon-size spiralized radishes look pretty in this salad, too, if your kids don't mind the peppery bite—my oldest loves it.

Real-Food Dole® Fruit Cup Copycat

(dairy-free, egg-free, gluten-free, nut-free, soy-free)

One year, my middle daughter had one of those store-bought fruit cups during a classroom birthday celebration. She was intrigued and of course adored that super sweet, fruity treat! She thought for sure we could buy some, because it's just fruit . . . right? After checking the ingredients list and discovering the sugary syrup overload, we decided to make our own. Grab some fun lidded containers and let the kids make their own fruit salad cups with fresh fruit, no refined sugar, and zero preservatives!

Makes 3 (½-cup [112-g]) servings

¾ cup (180 ml) water

¼ cup (60 ml) raw honey or pure maple syrup

1 tbsp (15 ml) fresh lime juice

½ cup (50 g) fresh blueberries

½ cup (98 g) fresh mandarin orange slices or pineapple chunks

1 cup (120 g) cubed fresh apples or pears

In a small bowl, whisk together the water, honey, and lime juice.

Stir the blueberries, mandarin orange slices, and apples into the honey-lime mixture. Divide the fruit and juice between 4-ounce (112-g), 6-ounce (168-g), or 8-ounce (224-g) storage cups with lids, depending on your child's serving size. Be sure the fruit is covered in the juice, so that the lime juice can prevent the apples from browning.

Notes

- Ball® brand makes 4-ounce (112-g), 6-ounce (168-g), and 8-ounce (224-g) freezer-safe containers with lids that work well for this recipe. For lunch-packing, I like using the leakproof round containers that my girls' PlanetBox lunchboxes came with.

- If your child doesn't like fruits that are mixed together (one of mine doesn't), you can use just one type of fruit. Cherries, peaches, pears, and pineapple work well in these fruit cups. Use whatever is in season or on sale where you live.

- You can double or triple this recipe to store in the refrigerator for up to 2 weeks for easy grab-and-go snacks.

Party Time Confetti Bean Salad

(dairy-free option, gluten-free, nut-free, soy-free)

Sprinkle this Italian-inspired salad with a "confetti" variety of protein-rich beans to fill the kids up for the afternoon! This cool, crisp salad, with its creamy beans and kid-friendly Italian dressing, is a perfect cold meal for those hot days near the end of the school year and during those first few weeks of school when it still feels like summer.

Makes 5 to 6 (2-cup [480-g]) servings

Creamy Italian Dressing

¾ cup (180 ml) olive or avocado oil

1 tbsp (15 ml) water

2 tbsp (30 ml) white wine vinegar

2 tbsp (28 g) mayonnaise of choice (such as Easy Homemade Mayo Two Ways [page 159], or store-bought avocado or olive oil mayo like Sir Kensington's or Chosen Foods brands)

1 tbsp (15 ml) raw honey

1 tsp garlic powder

¾ tsp onion powder

¾ tsp dried oregano

¾ tsp dried parsley

½ tsp sea salt, or as needed

Salad

1 medium head romaine lettuce, coarsely chopped

1 to 2 cups (200 to 400 g) cherry tomatoes, halved if they are large

1 cup (135 g) thawed frozen 1-inch (2.5-cm) green bean pieces

½ cup (83 g) home-cooked chickpeas (page 163)

½ cup (90 g) home-cooked navy beans or white kidney beans (page 163)

½ cup (30 g) cooked black beans (page 163)

½ cup (64 g) halved olives

Slivered sweet onions, as needed

Shaved Parmesan cheese, as needed (optional)

Sea salt, as needed

Black pepper, as needed

To make the Creamy Italian Dressing, combine the oil, water, vinegar, mayonnaise, honey, garlic powder, onion powder, oregano, parsley, and sea salt in a pint-sized (475-ml) Mason jar. Blend the ingredients with an immersion blender until they are smooth and creamy. This dressing lasts for 2 weeks in the refrigerator, so it can be made ahead of time.

To make the salad, toss together the lettuce, tomatoes, green beans, chickpeas, navy beans, black beans, olives, onions, Parmesan cheese (if using), and ½ cup (120 ml) of the Creamy Italian Dressing in a large bowl. Taste the salad and add the sea salt and black pepper if needed. To pack the salad in a lunchbox, pack the undressed salad with a condiment container of dressing.

Kid-Approved Broccoli Pesto Pasta Salad

(egg-free, gluten-free, nut-free option, soy-free)

Load up their lunchboxes with hidden mineral-rich broccoli and three different brain-boosting fats in a fun, kid-pleasing presentation: pasta! Whether it's served warm or cold, they'll be asking for this pasta salad over and over again.

Makes 8 to 9 (1-cup [200-g]) servings (younger kids will likely eat ½-cup [100-g] servings)

2 cups (350 g) broccoli florets

2 cloves garlic

½ cup (120 ml) plus 1 tbsp (15 ml) olive oil, divided

¾ to 1 tsp sea salt, divided

12 oz (336 g) uncooked gluten-free pasta (such as Jovial or Tinkyáda® brands)

1 cup (24 g) lightly packed fresh basil leaves

½ cup (60 g) walnuts or ¼ cup (32 g) raw unsalted sunflower seeds

½ cup (60 g) shredded raw cheese (see Notes)

Preheat the oven to 400°F (204°C). Line a large baking sheet with a silicone baking mat or unbleached parchment paper. Bring a large pot of water to a boil while the oven preheats.

Toss the broccoli and garlic with 1 tablespoon (15 ml) of the oil and ¼ teaspoon of the sea salt on the baking sheet. Roast the broccoli for 13 minutes, until the broccoli has softened but still has some bite to it.

While the broccoli is roasting, add the pasta to the boiling water and cook it per package directions. Drain the pasta and set it aside.

Combine the broccoli and garlic, basil, walnuts, and the remaining ½ to ¾ teaspoon of sea salt in a food processor. Pulse to process the ingredients into evenly distributed bits. Add the cheese and put the lid back on the food processor. With the food processor running, slowly drizzle in the remaining ½ cup (120 ml) of oil through the hole in the food processor's lid. Process until the pesto is smooth, stopping the food processor and scraping down the sides of the bowl once to ensure all the ingredients are incorporated.

Toss the broccoli pesto with the cooked pasta while it is still hot so that the pasta absorbs the oil. You can eat this pasta warm or cold. If your kids enjoy it better warm, use a thermos for lunch-packing.

The pasta salad lasts for up to 3 days in the refrigerator.

Notes
- Parmesan works well in this recipe, too, but back off on the sea salt a bit.
- When choosing a pasta shape, remember that smaller pastas, such as corkscrew, elbow, or bow tie, are easier for kids to manage in a lunchbox.

The Finishing Touches
Snacks and Sides

Easy to make, fun to eat, and quick to pack! Sometimes you just need a little lunchbox filler to complement that sandwich, salad, or soup. This section is all about snacks and sides to fill in the missing pieces to your lunchbox puzzle. For instance, let's say you spent the evening making a beautiful squash soup for dinner, saving the leftovers to pack for lunchboxes the next day, but you're wondering what to pack with it. Pull some Lightning-Fast Blender Batter Applesauce Muffins (page 130) from the freezer or a Crunchy Honey-Oat Nature Valley™ Granola Bar Copycat (page 121) from the pantry to fill in those lunchbox gaps. Or maybe you just need a quick handful of salty-sweet, protein-filled, healthy fat–rich Fast-Prep Healthy Trail Mix (page 125) to round out a lunchbox salad.

From Chewy Apple-Raisin Granola Bars (page 126) for morning snacks to Easy-Prep Sheet Pan Sweet Potato Tots (page 118), these healthy snacks and sides will become your secret stashes to pull from in a pinch!

How to Pack These Snacks and Sides for a Balanced Lunchbox

These snacks and sides are meant to be finishing touches to go alongside anything from sandwiches to soups. Some of the snacks are rich in protein and fat, like the Chewy Apple-Raisin Granola Bars (page 126). Other sides are a great source of energy-rich carbohydrates, like the Power-Packed Apricot Energy Bars (page 137). My suggestion in using this part of the book would be to plan one or two of these recipes into your prep day and start building your pantry and freezer stashes.

You'll also find these snacks and sides to be helpful to fill in the elusive morning snack at school that so many of us have to pack. While I (absolutely shamelessly!) use healthier, store-bought packaged snacks for the school morning snack a couple days per week, it saves my budget and brings some variety to my kids' diets to have homemade snacks on hand.

Easy-Prep Sheet Pan Sweet Potato Tots

(dairy-free, gluten-free, grain-free option, nut-free, soy-free)

Crispy on the outside, soft and sweet on the inside, these sweet potato tots are a fun way to add antioxidant-rich, vitamin-loaded sweet potatoes into your kids' lunchboxes. This no-fuss method makes a fun project to work on with the kids too.

Makes 45 to 50 sweet potato tots

Avocado or olive oil spray

2 lbs (900 g) sweet potatoes, peeled or unpeeled

1 tbsp (15 ml) olive oil

2 large eggs

1 cup (150 g) white rice flour or cassava flour or potato starch for grain-free

2 tsp (10 g) sea salt

1 tsp garlic powder

1 tsp onion powder

Preheat the oven to 375°F (191°C). Fit a large baking sheet with a baking rack. Spray the rack with the oil spray (or use a paper towel to rub the baking rack with avocado or olive oil).

Cut the ends off the sweet potatoes, cut the sweet potatoes into fourths, and place them in a food processor. Pulse the sweet potatoes until they are about the size of grains of rice.

Heat the oil in a large skillet over medium heat. Add the sweet potatoes. Cook the sweet potatoes for 5 to 7 minutes, stirring them every minute or so, until they are soft.

While the sweet potatoes are cooking, combine the eggs, flour, sea salt, garlic powder, and onion powder in a medium bowl. When the sweet potatoes are done cooking, add them to the egg mixture and stir to combine. Gently roll about 2 tablespoons (30 g) of the sweet potato mixture in your hands and use your thumbs and pointer fingers to create a square, 1½- to 2-inch (4- to 5-cm) "tot" shape. Place the tots on the prepared baking sheet.

Bake the sweet potato tots for 35 to 40 minutes (depending on the size tots you make), or until they are slightly crispy on the outside and lightly browned. When using the baking rack, there is no need to turn the tots or flip them. If you don't have a baking rack, you can bake them directly on the baking sheet, but you will have to turn the tots every 10 minutes to prevent burning the bottoms.

Note

- Freeze unbaked tots on the baking sheet for at least 1 hour. Transfer them to a freezer-safe bag. You can bake the frozen tots at 375°F (191°C), adding an extra 10 minutes to account for the thawing. To freeze baked tots, let them cool completely, and then transfer them to a freezer-safe bag.

Crunchy Honey-Oat Nature Valley™ Granola Bar Copycat

(dairy-free, egg-free, gluten-free, nut-free, soy-free)

One of my girls came home from school one day and told me she tried a friend's granola bar that she really wanted me to buy. After she described the package, the signature crunch, and the taste, I knew it was a Nature Valley™ bar she'd sampled. We did a quick scan of the ingredients, and, wanting to avoid the canola oil and processed syrups, we ran to the kitchen to make our own. Between the super-easy method and convenient pantry storage, you'll never miss the green box from the store, and you can feel better about the ingredients in these copycats!

Makes 8 bars or 16 square "bites"

2½ cups (200 g) rolled oats (do not use quick oats), divided

¼ cup (48 g) coconut sugar

¼ tsp sea salt

¼ tsp baking soda

¼ cup (60 g) coconut oil, melted, mixed with ¼ cup (60 ml) raw honey

Preheat the oven to 350°F (177°C). Line an 8 x 8-inch (20 x 20-cm) baking pan with unbleached parchment paper.

Use a blender or food processor to grind ½ cup (40 g) of the oats to make oat flour. Transfer the oat flour to a small bowl. Add the remaining 2 cups (160 g) of oats, sugar, sea salt, and baking soda to the oat flour. Pour the oil-honey mixture into the oat mixture and stir until everything is well combined.

Press the oat mixture into the prepared pan, using the bottom of a measuring cup to press the mixture into the sides.

Bake the granola for 20 minutes, until it is golden brown. It will feel soft while it is still hot. Remove the granola from the oven and let it cool in the cake pan for 10 minutes before pulling it out using the parchment paper and placing it on a baking rack to cool completely. Do not cut the bars until the granola has cooled to room temperature. The bars will be soft, but they will become crunchy as they cool.

These bars keep well in an airtight container in the pantry for up to 3 months, or they can be frozen for up to 6 months.

Note
- You can find sprouted oats, which are best for digestion, on Amazon and in many health-food stores.

Chocolate-Covered Banana Energy Bites

(dairy-free, egg-free, gluten-free, nut-free, soy-free)

Chocolate-covered bananas? Yes, please! These delicious bites are packed with protein and sweetened only with fruit. Cacao nibs are little bits of real cocoa bean before sugar is added to make chocolate. They are a great source of antioxidants, and when you mix them with the natural sweetness of the dates and bananas, the result tastes like sweetened chocolate. These little guys are a fun lunchbox addition that you can easily store in the pantry just like any store-bought lunchbox snack.

Makes 24 energy bites

1½ cups (113 g) Medjool dates, pitted

1 cup (128 g) raw unsalted sunflower seeds

1 tbsp (11 g) chia seeds

¼ tsp sea salt

¼ cup (17 g) banana chips

¼ cup (40 g) cacao nibs

Combine the dates, sunflower seeds, chia seeds, sea salt, and banana chips in a food processor and process until the mixture sticks together, about 1 minute. You may need to stop the food processor to scrape down the sides of the bowl occasionally.

Add the cacao nibs and process the mixture to combine. Roll the mixture into 2-inch (5-cm) energy bites. Store the energy bites in an airtight container in the pantry or refrigerator for up to 3 months.

Note
- If you can have nuts and are not in a nut-free school zone, you can swap the sunflower seeds for almonds or walnuts.

Fast-Prep Healthy Trail Mix

(dairy-free option, gluten-free, egg-free, nut-free option, soy-free)

Keep the pantry stocked with a jar of this easy-to-grab lunchbox trail mix! With fun pops of color and sweetness from the dried fruit, plus coconut and seeds (or nuts if you can have them) that balance blood sugar and keep kids full, this crunchy lunchbox snack is both satisfying and delicious.

Makes 8 cups (1 kg) trail mix

5 cups (600 g) nuts and/or seeds of choice (see Notes)

2 cups (300 g) dried fruit of choice (see Notes)

1 cup (75 g) unsweetened coconut flakes

3 tbsp (45 ml) melted butter or coconut oil

¼ to 1 tsp sea salt, or as needed (see Notes)

¼ to ½ cup (40 to 80 g) cacao nibs

Preheat the oven to 300°F (149°C). Set out two large baking sheets. Do not line or grease them.

Toss together the nuts, dried fruit, coconut flakes, melted butter, and sea salt on one of the baking sheets, and then divide the mixture evenly between that baking sheet and the second.

Bake the trail mix for 10 minutes. Stir the trail mix and then bake it for 5 to 7 minutes.

Cool the trail mix to room temperature, and then toss the trail mix with the cacao nibs.

Store the trail mix in an airtight container in the pantry for up to 6 months.

Notes

- If you can have them, here are some ideas: raw pumpkin seeds, raw unsalted sunflower seeds, flaxseeds, hemp hearts, almonds, pecans, brazil nuts, macadamia nuts, pistachios, walnuts, and peanuts. I like to use at least four different kinds of nuts or seeds to include a variety of nutrients and flavor! If you are in a nut-free school or classroom, please leave out the nuts.

- Try these dried fruits: raisins, apples, mangoes, cranberries, blueberries, goji berries, cherries, and pineapple. I like to include at least two different dried fruits for variety. Banana chips are another great addition to this recipe. Add them when you add the cacao nibs.

- If your nuts or seeds are salted, use just ¼ teaspoon of sea salt.

Chewy Apple-Raisin Granola Bars

(dairy-free, egg-free, gluten-free, nut-free option, soy-free)

Sweet apples and yummy raisins are sprinkled throughout these chewy granola bars, perfect for a midmorning snack or lunchbox side. And there's nothing to worry about if you are in a nut-free school zone, because these Quaker™-style granola bars can be made without nuts. These pantry-staple bars are filled with healthy, satiating fat and protein, and they have a delicious, kid-friendly taste.

Makes 12 bars

1 cup (90 g) dried apple

¾ cup (113 g) raisins, divided

¼ cup (43 g) chia seeds

½ cup (120 ml) melted coconut oil

¼ cup (60 ml) raw honey

¼ tsp sea salt (omit if your nuts or seeds are salted)

1½ cups (120 g) rolled oats (not quick oats)

1 cup (120 g) walnuts (see Notes)

½ cup (64 g) raw unsalted sunflower seeds

Preheat the oven to 325°F (163°C). Line an 8 x 8–inch (20 x 20–cm) baking pan with unbleached parchment paper.

Combine the apple, ½ cup (75 g) of the raisins, chia seeds, oil, honey, and sea salt in a food processor. Process to combine the ingredients. The mixture will have the texture of a sticky paste, which will help everything stick together.

Add the remaining ¼ cup (38 g) of the raisins, oats, walnuts, and sunflower seeds and pulse just a few seconds to combine. Scrape down the sides of the food processor's bowl and pulse a few more times, but do not let the mixture become completely smooth. Transfer the mixture to a medium bowl and combine the ingredients evenly with a rubber spatula.

Press the granola mixture evenly into the prepared baking pan using the bottom of a measuring cup. Bake the granola for 25 minutes, until the top is golden brown.

Cool the granola in the baking pan until it is cool enough to place in the refrigerator. Once the granola is cooled completely, cut it into bars. Store them in an airtight container in the pantry for 1 month or freeze them in a freezer-safe bag for up to 3 months.

Notes

- To make this recipe nut-free, swap the walnuts for ¾ cup (96 g) of raw unsalted sunflower seeds, and swap the ½ cup (64 g) of sunflower seeds for ½ cup (56 g) of raw pumpkin seeds. Flaxseeds would be fine here too.

- Golden raisins and white chia seeds are suitable swaps if you want a lighter color to your granola bars. I use the regular varieties of chia and raisins since those are more readily available.

Real-Food KIND® Bar Copycat

(dairy-free, egg-free, gluten-free, nut-free option, soy-free)

Skip the glucose syrups, milk powders, junky oils, and other fillers in the store-bought KIND® bars! You'll be shocked at how simple it is to make your own, and the kids will be thrilled that they taste just like the bars at the store. These easy-prep bars make for fast lunchbox fillers, and they can be made safe for nut-free school zones with the all-seed version.

Makes 12 bars

1¼ cups (213 g) raw almonds (see Notes)

¼ cup (32 g) raw unsalted sunflower seeds

¼ cup (28 g) raw pumpkin seeds

¼ cup (19 g) unsweetened shredded coconut

1 tbsp (13 g) hulled millet

¼ cup (60 ml) pure maple syrup

¼ to ½ tsp sea salt

Preheat the oven to 325°F (163°C). Line an 8 x 8-inch (20 x 20–cm) baking dish with unbleached parchment paper.

In a small bowl, stir together the almonds, sunflower seeds, pumpkin seeds, coconut, millet, maple syrup, and sea salt until the ingredients are well combined. Use the bottom of a measuring cup to press the mixture evenly into the prepared baking dish.

Bake the mixture for 35 minutes, until the top is lightly toasted. Let the bar mixture cool in the baking dish for at least 1 hour, or until they reach room temperature. Do not disturb it during this time or it will not harden. When you are ready to cut it, use the parchment paper to pull the solid square out of the pan, and use a long, sharp knife to cut the square into bars of your desired size.

Wrap the bars individually in parchment paper, and then store them in an airtight container for up to 1 month in the pantry or store them in the freezer for up to 6 months.

Notes

- For the nut-free, seed-based version, use 1¼ cups (160 g) of raw unsalted sunflower seeds, ½ cup (56 g) of raw pumpkin seeds, ¼ cup (19 g) of unsweetened shredded coconut, 1 tablespoon (7 g) of flaxseed meal, 1 tablespoon (13 g) of hulled millet, ¼ cup (60 ml) of maple syrup, and ½ teaspoon of sea salt. The method is the same.

- An 8 x 8-inch (20 x 20–cm) square cake pan will give you the sharpest edges on the outside of the bars. A square casserole dish works fine if that is all you have, but the more rounded corners will leave that part of the bars more rounded.

Lightning-Fast Blender
Batter Applesauce Muffins

(dairy-free, gluten-free, nut-free, soy-free)

These soft, delicious muffins will become a regular staple in your lunchbox rotation after you see how quick and easy the prep is—and how fast the kids make them disappear! Packed with friendly fats for nervous system nourishment and the kid-friendly flavors of apple and honey, these little lunchbox fillers go great with everything from a thermos of soup to a salad.

Makes 12 muffins

½ cup (123 g) unsweetened applesauce

4 large eggs

½ cup (120 ml) olive or avocado oil

2 to 3 tbsp (30 to 45 ml) raw honey

½ cup (56 g) coconut flour

¼ cup (40 g) tapioca starch

½ tsp baking soda

¼ tsp sea salt

½ tsp ground cinnamon

Preheat the oven to 375°F (191°C). Line a muffin pan with unbleached paper liners or silicone muffin cup liners.

In a blender or food processor, combine the applesauce, eggs, oil, honey, flour, tapioca starch, baking soda, sea salt, and cinnamon. Blend until the ingredients form a smooth batter.

Pour the batter into the prepared muffin pan. Bake the muffins for 20 minutes, until they are golden brown and spring back when touched.

Let the muffins cool for 5 minutes in the pan before transferring them to a baking rack to cool completely. Muffins will last 3 days at room temperature.

To freeze the muffins, let them cool completely before putting them into a freezer-safe bag for up to 3 months. You can pull the frozen muffins out of the freezer and pack them in the lunchbox—they should be thawed by lunchtime.

Note
- The recipe as written with the 2 to 3 tablespoons (30 to 45 ml) of honey makes these muffins mildly sweet, which is great for little kids. But if your older children are used to sweeter food, you may want to bump the honey up to 4 tablespoons (60 ml).

Savory Garlic Bread Muffins

(gluten-free, nut-free, soy-free)

Cheesy, buttery, soft, and savory: What's not to love? Add these easy-to-grab muffins to any lunch that you would eat with a piece of garlic bread! Whether you're packing your kids a loaded salad or a thermos of spaghetti or soup, these fluffy muffins will be the request of your kids week after week.

Makes 12 muffins

2 large eggs

4 tbsp (60 g) unsalted butter, melted

1 tbsp (12 g) coconut sugar, maple sugar, turbinado sugar, or rapadura sugar

1 cup (240 ml) buttermilk or coconut buttermilk (see Notes)

1 cup (122 g) Namaste Perfect Flour Blend

2 tsp (8 g) aluminum-free baking powder

½ tsp sea salt

½ tsp garlic powder

1 cup (120 g) shredded cheese

Preheat the oven to 400°F (204°C). Line a muffin pan with unbleached paper muffin liners or silicone muffin cup liners.

In a medium bowl, combine the eggs, butter, and sugar. Mix the ingredients together for 1 minute using a handheld mixer.

Add the buttermilk, flour, baking powder, sea salt, and garlic powder and blend to combine. Fold in the cheese and scoop the batter into the prepared muffin pan.

Bake the muffins for 20 minutes, until they spring back when touched and are golden brown. Let the muffins cool in the pan for 5 minutes, then transfer them to a baking rack to cool completely. Muffins will last 3 days at room temperature.

To freeze the muffins, let them cool completely before putting them into a freezer-safe bag. You can pull the frozen muffins out of the freezer and pack them in the lunchbox—they should be thawed by lunchtime. Muffins will last 3 months in the freezer.

Notes

- To make 1 cup (240 ml) buttermilk, put 1 tablespoon (15 ml) of apple cider vinegar in a liquid measuring cup and fill the measuring to the 1-cup (240-ml) mark with coconut milk or raw milk.

- Use whatever cheese you have in the house—I've used multiple kinds and they all turn out great. Even goat cheese and a sheep's cheese like Manchego work.

Sweet Cinnamon Top-Secret Veggie Mini Muffins

(dairy-free, gluten-free, nut-free, soy-free)

These quick-prep blender muffins will be the star of the show in any lunchbox or snack box with their soft, bread-like texture and warm, sweet cinnamon flavor. Even your most top-secret veggie detective is sure to happily gobble up these mini muffins!

Makes 36 mini muffins (or 12 to 16 regular muffins)

Avocado or olive oil spray, as needed

1 medium carrot, peeled or unpeeled and coarsely chopped

1 medium zucchini, coarsely chopped

3 large eggs

⅓ cup (80 ml) olive or avocado oil

¼ cup (71 g) full-fat coconut yogurt or dairy yogurt (see Notes)

⅓ cup (64 g) coconut sugar, turbinado sugar, rapadura sugar, or maple sugar

1 tbsp (15 ml) apple cider vinegar

2 tsp (10 ml) pure vanilla extract

1 cup (140 g) Otto's brand cassava flour

1 tbsp (9 g) ground cinnamon

1 tsp aluminum-free baking powder

1 tsp baking soda

¼ tsp sea salt

Preheat the oven to 350°F (177°C). Spray a mini muffin pan with the oil spray.

Put the carrot and zucchini in a food processor. Pulse until the veggies are pieces similar in size to sesame seeds. (You may have to scrape down the food processor's bowl between pulses.)

Add the eggs, oil, yogurt, sugar, vinegar, vanilla, flour, cinnamon, baking powder, baking soda, and sea salt. Process to combine the ingredients well, scraping down the sides of the food processor's bowl occasionally to be sure everything is incorporated.

Scoop the muffin batter into the prepared muffin pan, filling each muffin cup most of the way. Bake the muffins for 20 to 24 minutes, until the tops are golden brown and the muffins spring back when touched. If you make the muffins in a regular muffin pan, plan to add 5 to 10 more minutes to the baking time. Cool the muffins in the pan for 10 minutes, and then transfer them to a baking rack to cool completely.

To freeze the muffins, let them cool completely before putting them into a freezer-safe bag for up to 3 months. You can pull the frozen muffins out of the freezer and pack them in the lunchbox— they should be thawed by lunchtime.

Notes

- When I was testing this recipe for this book, I measured the amount of veggies I was cutting each time I made these muffins, since veggies can vary in size. For your reference, the amount of chopped vegetables came to 3 cups (450 g).

- If you don't have access to coconut yogurt, full-fat coconut milk or dairy milk would work too.

Power-Packed Apricot Energy Bars

(dairy-free, egg-free, gluten-free, nut-free, soy-free)

Give them a little boost of energy for the school afternoon or that after-school sport with these little apricot-sweetened bars! The gooey, fig bar–like middle and crunchy crust makes for a kid favorite that they will ask for over and over—and you can feel good about the ingredients compared to store-bought energy bars that are loaded with sugar, preservatives, and questionable flavorings.

Makes 16 (2-inch [5-cm]) energy bars or 9 (3-inch [7.5-cm]) energy bars

½ cup (120 g) coconut oil, melted, plus more as needed

1 cup (150 g) dried apricots

½ cup (120 ml) water

1½ cups (120 g) rolled oats (do not use quick oats)

½ cup (80 g) tapioca starch

⅓ cup (40 g) buckwheat flour

¼ cup (26 g) flaxseed meal

¼ cup (48 g) coconut sugar

½ tsp baking soda

¼ tsp sea salt

Preheat the oven to 350°F (177°C). Grease an 8 x 8–inch (20 x 20–cm) cake pan or baking dish with the additional oil.

Put the apricots and water in a small saucepan over high heat. Bring the apricots to a simmer, reduce the heat to medium, and cook the apricots for 10 minutes while you prepare the crust.

In a medium bowl, whisk together the oats, tapioca starch, flour, flaxseed meal, sugar, baking soda, and sea salt. Stir in the melted coconut oil with a rubber spatula until the ingredients are combined.

Scoop out 1 cup (240 g) of the crust mixture and set it aside for the top of the bars. Put the rest of the crust mixture in the bottom of the prepared cake pan and press it down with the rubber spatula.

Transfer the apricots and water to a blender and blend the mixture to a puree (you can add 1 tablespoon [15 ml] of water if the blender is having a hard time blending the thick, jam-like mixture). Spread the apricot filling over the crust with the rubber spatula.

Sprinkle the remaining 1 cup (240 g) of the crust mixture over the top of the apricot filling, using the rubber spatula to gently spread and press the top crust down into the apricot filling.

Bake the bar mixture for 25 minutes, until the edges are golden brown. Let the mixture cool slightly in the pan, then transfer the pan to the refrigerator to cool completely. Cut the mixture into bars.

These bars freeze well. Let them cool completely, and cut them into the desired size. Freeze the bars in freezer-safe bags for up to 3 months. You can pull them from the freezer to pack in the lunchboxes—they will be thawed by lunchtime.

Lunchbox Treats

From birthdays to the holidays, it's time to celebrate!

And it is absolutely okay to include a bit of that celebration with a little lunchbox treat here and there. I want my kids (and yours) to have a healthy relationship with any and all food. From salads to treats and everything in between. Part of that mission is giving children a picture of what balance means. Balance is a mini birthday cupcake in your lunchbox on your special day. Balance is a few fun gummy bears the day after Halloween when all your friends are bringing in a fun-size bag of Skittles® from their trick-or-treating adventures. And balance is sometimes popping a yummy fruit roll-up in their lunchbox on a random Wednesday just to make them smile! It's all part of helping children create a healthy relationship with food. When you take the "forbidden" out of the treats, kids learn how to celebrate in a healthy way and enjoy their food in the process.

How to Pack These Lunchbox Treats for a Balanced Lunchbox

Lunchbox treats are just that: treats! So these fun bits and bites will be additions to an already full and balanced lunchbox. Simply build your lunchbox with a good balance of protein, fat, and healthy carbohydrates, then pop in a Fall-Favorite Pumpkin Cookie (page 143) for that harvest party or a Valentine's Day Brownie Bite (page 147) on the day that the classroom is celebrating Valentine's Day.

Fresh Fruit-Packed Gummy Bears

(dairy-free, egg-free, gluten-free, nut-free, soy-free)

Nothing spooky about these gummy bear look-alikes! When those Halloween bags are piled high with candy, send along a wholesome version of gummy bears in their lunchbox the next day. Instead of fake food dyes and gobs of sugar, your kids can enjoy a special treat packed with fresh fruit, honey, and protein-packed gelatin.

Makes 4 servings (number of bears will depend on the size of mold)

1½ cups (360 g) fresh fruit or thawed and drained frozen fruit of choice (see Notes)

2 tbsp (30 ml) water

2 tbsp (30 ml) raw honey, plus more as needed

2 tbsp (28 g) grass-fed gelatin

Put the fruit and water in a small saucepan over medium heat. Bring the mixture to a simmer and cook the fruit for 3 to 4 minutes.

Transfer the warm fruit and cooking liquid to a blender. Add the honey and gelatin and blend until the mixture is smooth. Taste the mixture and add more honey if needed.

Pour the fruit-gelatin mixture into a gummy bear mold and place the mold in the freezer for 15 to 30 minutes. I find that the gummy bears pop out of silicone molds easiest when they are slightly frozen. Alternatively, you can let them gel at room temperature—depending on the size of your mold, it will take about 1 hour. You can also chill the gummy bears in the refrigerator for about 30 minutes.

The gummy bears will hold their shape at room temperature in a lunchbox. Store them in the refrigerator since they are made with fresh fruit. They will keep for about 1 week in the refrigerator.

Notes

- If the fruit is out of season and not as sweet, you may bump up the honey a bit. For younger children, you could get away with less honey.
- For Halloween, peaches or mangoes make a great orange color. Strawberries, raspberries, and cherries make fantastic hues of red. Blueberries are a pretty purple once the gelatin is set. Larger fruit, like strawberries and peaches, should be chopped before measuring. Harder fruits, like apples or pears, should work well but will need to cook about 5 minutes longer to soften completely. Bananas do not work well for this recipe.

Fall-Favorite Pumpkin Cookies

(dairy-free, gluten-free, nut-free, soy-free)

From Halloween to harvest days, the kids will love these soft, bite-size pumpkin cookies for any of their special autumn classroom parties! They'll feel so special to have a little treat in their lunchbox on a fun day, and you'll feel good about the real-food ingredients and easy prep.

Makes 36 mini lunchbox cookies or 18 larger cookies

¼ cup (60 g) coconut oil, melted

½ cup (96 g) coconut sugar, maple sugar, turbinado sugar, rapadura sugar, or organic cane sugar

¼ cup (56 g) pumpkin puree

1 large egg

2 tsp (10 ml) blackstrap molasses

1 tsp pure vanilla extract

1½ cups (240 g) tapioca starch

2 tbsp (14 g) coconut flour

1 tsp pumpkin pie spice or ground cinnamon

½ tsp aluminum-free baking powder

Preheat the oven to 325°F (163°C). Line a large baking sheet with a silicone baking mat or unbleached parchment paper.

In a medium bowl, use a handheld mixer to combine the oil, sugar, pumpkin puree, egg, molasses, and vanilla until the mixture is smooth.

Add the tapioca starch, flour, pumpkin pie spice, and baking powder and blend until the mixture is well combined. Cover the bowl and refrigerate it for at least 30 minutes.

Scoop approximately 1 tablespoon (15 g) of the chilled dough from the bowl, roll it into a ball, place it on the prepared baking sheet, and gently press down on the cookie. Do not flatten the dough — just press it down a little. The cookies will spread out more as they bake. Repeat this process with the remaining cookie dough.

Bake the pumpkin cookies for 12 minutes, until they are golden brown. Cool the cookies on the baking sheet for 5 minutes before transferring them to a baking rack to cool completely.

To freeze the cookies, cool them completely and place them in a gallon freezer-safe bag. You can pull frozen cookies from the freezer and pack them right in the lunchbox — they will thaw by lunchtime. The cookies will last for up to 3 months in the freezer. The cookies will last for about 5 days at room temperature or for up to 2 weeks in the refrigerator.

Note

- A sprinkle of organic powdered sugar or a schmear of cream cheese frosting would be fun on these cookies too!

Gingerbread Bites

(dairy-free option, gluten-free, nut-free, soy-free)

Add a little sweet treat to their lunchbox during that last week of school before the holiday break. These fun, soft, and chewy gingerbread bites will bring all of their favorite holiday flavors to their lunchbox, filling the rest of their day with holiday cheer!

Makes 24 gingerbread bites

½ cup (120 g) softened butter or palm shortening

2 tbsp (30 ml) blackstrap molasses

⅓ cup (64 g) coconut sugar, maple sugar, turbinado sugar, rapadura sugar, or organic cane sugar

1 large egg

1¾ cups (214 g) Namaste Perfect Flour Blend, plus more as needed (see Notes)

1 tsp ground cinnamon

½ tsp ground ginger

¼ tsp ground cloves

¼ tsp ground nutmeg

¼ tsp sea salt

1 tsp baking soda

In a large bowl, use a handheld mixer to combine the butter, molasses, sugar, and egg until smooth.

Add the flour, cinnamon, ginger, cloves, nutmeg, sea salt, and baking soda and mix to combine. Chill the dough in the refrigerator for at least 1 hour.

Preheat the oven to 375°F (191°C). Line a large baking sheet with a silicone baking mat or unbleached parchment paper.

Sprinkle a work surface with some additional flour and roll the gingerbread dough out until it is ¼ inch (6 mm) thick. Use a mini gingerbread man cookie cutter to cut out the cookies. Place the gingerbread bites on the prepared baking sheet.

Bake the gingerbread bites for 8 minutes, until they are golden brown on top. Let them cool on the baking sheet for about 2 minutes, and then transfer them to a baking rack to cool completely.

To freeze the cookies, cool them completely and place them in a gallon freezer-safe bag. Store them in the freezer for up to 3 months. You can pull frozen cookies from the freezer and pack them right in the lunchbox—they will thaw by lunchtime. The cookies will last for about 5 days at room temperature or for up to 2 weeks in the refrigerator.

Notes

- Other gluten-free flour blends may work; however, results will vary if the ingredient blend is different. If using a different brand, you may need to adjust the amounts.
- A classic royal icing with powdered sugar would be a fun way to add a smile to your gingerbread man or lady!

Valentine's Day Brownie Bites

(dairy-free option, gluten-free, nut-free, soy-free)

Say "I love you" in the best way for Valentine's Day at school: with chocolate! These tiny brownie bites are sweet and rich, and they're just the perfect size for a school lunchbox. Leave them feeling loved without spiking their blood sugar for the afternoon with these decadent brownie bites.

Makes 24 brownie bites

Avocado or olive oil spray, as needed

2 large eggs

¼ cup (60 ml) olive oil

¼ cup (71 g) full-fat coconut yogurt or dairy yogurt

⅓ cup (64 g) coconut sugar

¼ cup (60 ml) raw honey

1 tsp pure vanilla extract

½ cup (61 g) Namaste Perfect Flour Blend (see Notes)

½ cup (55 g) unsweetened cocoa powder

¼ tsp baking soda

¼ tsp sea salt

Preheat the oven to 325°F (163°C). Spray a mini muffin pan with the oil spray.

In a large bowl, use a handheld mixer to combine the eggs, oil, yogurt, sugar, honey, and vanilla until the mixture is smooth and creamy.

Add the flour, cocoa powder, baking soda, and sea salt and mix on low speed until the batter is smooth, shiny, and fudgy.

Pour the batter into the prepared mini muffin pan. Bake the brownie bites for 12 minutes, until they spring back when touched.

To freeze the brownies, let them cool completely before transferring them to freezer-safe bags for up to 3 months. You can pull frozen brownie bites from the freezer and pack them right in the lunchbox—they will thaw by lunchtime.

Notes

- Other gluten-free flour blends may work; however, results will vary if the ingredient blend is different. If using a different brand, you may need to adjust the amounts.
- You can add mini chocolate chips to the batter if you want. If you like a salted brownie flavor, you can sprinkle the tops with coarse sea salt.

Blender Batter "Funfetti®" Mini Birthday Cupcakes

(dairy-free option, gluten-free, nut-free, soy-free)

Makes 12 mini cupcakes

¼ cup (60 g) softened butter or palm shortening

¼ cup (60 ml) raw honey

¼ cup (60 ml) full-fat milk or full-fat coconut milk

1 egg

½ tsp pure vanilla extract

¾ cup (92 g) Namaste Perfect Flour Blend (see Notes)

½ tsp aluminum-free baking powder

¼ tsp sea salt

1 tbsp (18 g) naturally dyed sprinkles (see Notes)

Preheat the oven to 350°F (177°C). Line a mini muffin pan with mini silicone cupcake liners or unbleached mini cupcake liners.

In a blender, combine the butter, honey, milk, egg, and vanilla. Blend the ingredients for 30 seconds on high speed. Add the flour, baking powder, and sea salt and blend until the batter is smooth.

Fold the sprinkles into the batter using a spoon, and then pour the cupcake batter into the cupcake liners.

Bake the mini cupcakes for 17 to 18 minutes, until the tops are light golden brown and they spring back when touched. Let the mini cupcakes cool in the pan for 5 minutes before transferring them to a baking rack to cool completely. To freeze the cupcakes, let them cool completely, then transfer them to a freezer-safe bag. They can be stored in the freezer for up to 3 months. You can pull frozen cupcakes from the freezer and pack them right in the lunchbox— they will thaw by lunchtime.

Notes

- Other gluten-free flour blends may work; however, results will vary if the ingredient blend is different. If using a different brand, you may need to adjust the amounts.

- I like ColorKitchen brand sprinkles, which many regular grocery stores carry.

Butter Cookie Cutouts for Any and Every Holiday

(egg-free, gluten-free, nut-free, soy-free)

Bake sweet little cookie shapes, no matter what the occasion! Mini cookie cutters were one of my most favorite discoveries as a new mom. From pumpkins to candy canes and valentine hearts to spring flowers, these little shortbread tea cookies have just the right amount of sweetness to feel like a treat without overdoing it like a sugar cookie.

Makes 12 regular-sized cutout cookies or 24 mini cutout cookies

½ cup (120 g) salted butter, softened

¼ cup (33 g) organic powdered sugar

½ tsp pure vanilla extract

1 cup (122 g) Namaste Perfect Flour Blend, plus more as needed (see Notes)

Preheat the oven to 350°F (177°C). Line a large baking sheet with a silicone baking mat or unbleached parchment paper.

Combine the butter, powdered sugar, and vanilla in a food processor and process to cream the ingredients together. Add the flour and process to combine until a dough forms.

Dust a work surface and rolling pin with additional flour. Transfer the dough to the work surface. Roll the dough out to the desired thickness (I recommend ⅛ inch [3 mm]), and cut out the shapes you want with cookie cutters.

Place the cookies on the prepared baking sheet. Bake mini cookies for 5 to 6 minutes or regular-sized cookies for 8 to 10 minutes, until the edges are just starting to become golden brown. (The baking time will also depend on how thick the cookies are.) Let the cookies cool for about 2 minutes on the baking sheet, and then transfer them to a baking rack to cool completely.

Store the cooled cookies in an airtight container for 2 days, or freeze them by cooling them completely before putting them in freezer-safe bags and freezing them for up to 3 months.

Notes

- Other gluten-free flour blends may work; however, results will vary if the ingredient blend is different. If using a different brand, you may need to adjust the amounts.
- You can sprinkle your cookies with naturally dyed sprinkles before baking them if you want.
- If you want to frost your cookies or dip them in chocolate, wait until they are completely cooled.

Real-Food Fruit Roll-Ups™ Copycat

(dairy-free, egg-free, gluten-free, nut-free, soy-free)

These Fruit Roll-Ups™ look-alikes are packed with whole fruit and all the fun flavor. They make a fun lunchbox treat any day of the week. You can feel good about being in the driver's seat to control the amount of honey to sweeten these little treats, and the kids will have so much fun unrolling their strips of fun!

Makes 8 to 10 fruit roll-ups

4 cups (576 g) hulled fresh strawberries (see Note)

1 tbsp (15 ml) fresh lemon juice

2 to 3 tbsp (30 to 45 ml) light-colored raw honey

Preheat the oven to the lowest possible setting—typically 170°F (77°C). Line a large baking sheet with a silicone baking mat. (Parchment paper works but is harder to work with in my experience.)

In a blender, combine the strawberries, lemon juice, and honey. Blend the ingredients into a very smooth puree. Spread the mixture over the silicone baking mat as evenly as possible. Bake the fruit mixture for about 3 hours, until it is dried out and not sticky to the touch.

Let the fruit roll-ups mixture cool completely, and then use a pizza cutter to slice the mixture into strips. The fruit roll-ups will not be sticky at first, but they will get a little tacky overnight, so I find that rolling the strips up with parchment paper is the best way to store them.

Note

- Use in-season fruit! This recipe works well with any summer fruit (such as raspberries, blueberries, peaches, and cherries) as well as applesauce in the fall. You can even do cooked butternut squash puree as a veggie roll-up—just add a bit more honey.

Real-Food Staples

When it comes to lunch-packing, everyone needs a few secret staples in their back pocket!

This bonus section of *The Little Lunchbox Cookbook* is my gift to you—I want you to feel empowered to take control of the ingredients in your daily lunch-packing. When kids are eating weekly condiments like ranch dressing, hummus, and mayo, you want to feel good about the ingredients they are consuming. With easy-to-prep salad dressings and dips, you can be in the driver's seat and make the ingredient decisions for your family. This chapter will also help you expand your meal-prep skills by teaching you how to save time and money by using a weekly whole chicken for multiple meals, making your own budget-friendly and nourishing bone broth for delicious soups and stews, and how to stock your freezer with easy-to-cook beans for protein additions to meals, soups, dips, and spreads.

Easy Homemade Ranch

(dairy-free option, egg-free, gluten-free, nut-free, soy-free)

Hidden Valley® has nothing on this real-food copycat! They will never miss the store-bought version, and you won't believe how fast you can make your own with nourishing ingredients that they will want to dip every veggie in.

Makes 2 cups (480 ml)

1¼ cups (150 g) full-fat sour cream

⅓ cup (80 ml) whole raw milk or full-fat coconut milk

Juice of ½ small lemon or 1 tsp white wine vinegar

1 tsp dried parsley

1½ tsp (5 g) onion powder

1 tsp garlic powder

½ to 1 tsp sea salt

½ tsp black pepper

In a pint-sized (475-ml) Mason jar, combine the sour cream, milk, lemon juice, parsley, onion powder, garlic powder, sea salt, and black pepper. Stir the dressing until it is smooth and well combined.

The dressing keeps in the refrigerator for 1 week.

Notes

- For a dairy-free version, a small avocado swaps well for the sour cream. You will have to use an immersion blender or a food processor to make the dressing. The dressing's color will be light green, but it definitely still tastes like ranch. I have also tried mayonnaise to swap for the sour cream, and while it does work, I prefer the taste of the avocado ranch.

- If you want a thicker ranch for dipping, you can leave out the milk or add only a few splashes. If you prefer a runnier dressing, you can add more milk.

Five-Minute Catalina Copycat

(dairy-free, egg-free, gluten-free, nut-free, soy-free)

From a simple lunchbox salad to your favorite topping to drizzle over tacos, you'll be blown away by the restaurant-quality flavor of this Catalina copycat. This dressing's prep couldn't get any faster, so feel free to pour it all over that salad.

Makes 2 cups (480 ml)

¾ cup (180 ml) olive or avocado oil

¼ cup (60 ml) white wine vinegar

⅓ cup (91 g) organic ketchup

Juice of ½ small lemon

2 to 3 tbsp (30 to 45 ml) raw honey

2 tsp (6 g) onion powder

1 tsp mustard powder

1 tsp smoked paprika

1 tsp sea salt

¼ to ½ tsp black pepper

In a pint-sized (475-ml) Mason jar, combine the oil, vinegar, ketchup, lemon juice, honey, onion powder, mustard powder, smoked paprika, sea salt, and black pepper. Blend the dressing with an immersion blender.

This dressing keeps in the refrigerator for 2 to 3 weeks.

Super Smooth Kid-Favorite Hummus

(dairy-free, egg-free, gluten-free, nut-free, soy-free)

Hummus is the busy mom's backup plan to quickly add protein and fat to their kids' lunchboxes! Scoop some hummus into any lunchbox condiment container, and the dipping vehicle ideas are endless, from carrot sticks and crinkle-cut cucumber rounds to crackers and pita bread slices.

Makes about 2 cups (490 g)

1 cup (165 g) canned or home-cooked chickpeas (page 163), drained and rinsed if needed

½ cup (120 ml) olive or avocado oil

2 tbsp (30 g) sunflower butter

½ to 1 tsp sea salt

1 clove garlic

Water, as needed (see Notes)

In a food processor or blender, combine the chickpeas, oil, sunflower butter, sea salt, garlic, and water. Process until the hummus is smooth.

Store the hummus in an airtight container in the refrigerator for about 1 week. Hummus freezes well, too, for up to 3 months in a freezer-safe container.

Notes

- I have found that my kids like the taste of hummus better using sunflower butter, but tahini would work great if your kids like that flavor.

- I like my hummus super smooth, so I use about ¼ cup (60 ml) of water.

Easy Homemade Mayo Two Ways

Now everyone can enjoy the nourishing benefits of homemade mayonnaise with these two recipes. Spread a thick layer on your favorite sandwich, or mix up as much as you want into that tuna salad or egg salad. These mayo recipes use only brain-nourishing fats, and they've got the fastest prep around!

Makes 2 cups (440 g)

Traditional Mayo
(dairy-free, gluten-free, nut-free, soy-free)

1 large egg

2 tsp (10 ml) white wine vinegar

2 tsp (6 g) mustard powder

1 to 2 tsp (4 to 8 g) organic cane sugar

¼ tsp garlic powder

½ tsp sea salt, or as needed

1 cup (240 ml) avocado or olive oil

In a quart-sized (946-ml) Mason jar, combine the egg, vinegar, mustard powder, sugar, garlic powder, sea salt, and oil. Put an immersion blender at the bottom of the jar and blend on low speed until you see white mayonnaise start to form—this takes only a few seconds. Increase the blender's speed to high and move the immersion blender up and down until the mayonnaise is thick and creamy. Transfer the mayo to a pint-sized (475-ml) Mason jar with a lid to store it in the refrigerator for up to 1 week.

Egg-Free Mayonnaise
(egg-free, gluten-free, nut-free, soy-free)

½ cup (120 ml) avocado or olive oil

½ cup (60 g) full-fat sour cream

2 tsp (10 ml) white wine vinegar

2 tsp (6 g) mustard powder

1 to 2 tsp (4 to 8 g) organic cane sugar

¼ tsp garlic powder

½ tsp sea salt

In a pint-sized (475-ml) Mason jar, combine the oil, sour cream, vinegar, mustard powder, sugar, garlic powder, and sea salt. Blend the ingredients with an immersion blender until the mayo is smooth and creamy. Store the mayo in the jar with its lid on for up to 1 week.

Note

- Please note that avocado oil has the most neutral flavor; therefore, it works well for a kid-friendly mayo. If you or the kids enjoy the taste of olive oil, you will enjoy the olive oil version!

Real-Food Staples   159

Quick and Easy
Freezer-Friendly Applesauce

(dairy-free, egg-free, gluten-free, nut-free, soy-free)

Applesauce is such a fun treat to add to a lunchbox—and this no-sugar-added recipe is fast and fun to make with the kids! We pick apples every autumn and stash away batches and batches of this applesauce so that we can add it to lunchboxes all year.

Makes 16 cups (3.9 L)

5 lbs (2.3 kg) apples, peeled or unpeeled and cored

1 cup (240 ml) water

Put the apples and water in the bottom of a slow cooker or an Instant Pot®. If you are using a slow cooker, place the lid on the slow cooker and cook the apples on low for 8 hours or on high for 4 hours.

If you are using an Instant Pot®, place the lid on the cooker and make sure the valve is closed. Press Manual and set the timer for 4 minutes. The Instant Pot® will start automatically, taking 5 to 10 minutes to come to pressure before counting down the 4 minutes. Release the pressure as soon as the cooking is finished.

You can use a manual food mill to process the cooked apples, which makes a very smooth applesauce. Or you can blend the apples in a high-powered blender until they are smooth.

To freeze the applesauce, let it cool completely before storing it in BPA-free freezer-safe containers for up to 3 months. The applesauce will last 1 week in the refrigerator.

Note
- You can add cinnamon to your taste if you enjoy cinnamon-spiced applesauce.

Probiotic-Rich Fermented Bread and Butter Pickles

(dairy-free, egg-free, gluten-free, nut-free, soy-free)

Sweet, crispy, crunchy . . . and loaded with naturally occurring probiotics for the gut's first line of defense! The kids will adore these mild bread and butter pickles in their sandwiches, wraps, salads, and even alone as a yummy veggie side dish.

Makes 1 pint (306 g)

1½ to 2 small salad cucumbers, sliced into rounds with a crinkle cutter or knife

1 clove garlic

1½ tsp (8 g) sea salt

2 tsp (6 g) mustard seeds

1 tbsp (15 ml) pure maple syrup

Water, as needed

Stuff as many cucumbers as you can into a pint-sized (475-ml) Mason jar or pint-sized (475-ml) Fido jar with a clamp lid, leaving 1½ to 2 inches (4 to 5 cm) of space at the top of the jar.

Add the garlic, sea salt, mustard seeds, and maple syrup. Fill the jar with water to cover the cucumbers. If you have a fermenting weight, place that on top of the cucumbers to keep them submerged in the water. If you do not have a weight, you can just fill the jar with extra water to ensure that the cucumbers don't come out of the water.

Put a plastic Mason jar lid on the jar, use a Pickle Pipe® (which is what I use), or close the sealed latch lid of the Fido jar. If you use a Pickle Pipe®, your jar will let the gasses out automatically. If you are using a plastic lid or a Fido jar, "burp" your jar every day to let the gasses out: Open the lid slightly to let the gasses escape, then tighten the lid again. Leave the cucumbers to ferment at room temperature for at least 5 days or up to 1 week or more, depending on how strong you like the taste of your pickles—the longer they ferment, the more sour they will become. If your home is very warm, they will ferment faster.

The pickles will last 6 months in the refrigerator.

Note
- This recipe will double into a quart-sized (946-ml) Mason jar if you want to make a bigger batch.

Weekly Staple Hard-Boiled Eggs

(dairy-free, gluten-free, nut-free, soy-free)

Hard-boiled eggs became a weekly staple in my weekend prep-day routine when my girls were very little. Having a dozen hard-boiled eggs ready to go in the fridge at all times means healthy, grab-and-go snacks, easy lunchbox fillers, and quick egg salad anytime!

Makes 3 to 12 hard-boiled eggs

Water, as needed

3 to 12 large eggs (see Notes)

Notes

- Be sure that no matter which cooking method you are using that the eggs aren't overcrowded.

- Hard-boiled eggs keep for 5 days in the refrigerator.

Instant Pot® Method

Put 1 cup (240 ml) of water in the bottom of the Instant Pot®. Place the trivet at the bottom of the Instant Pot®, and place 3 to 12 eggs on top of the trivet.

Put the lid on the Instant Pot®, close the valve, and press Manual. Set the pressure to low and set the timer for 4 minutes. The Instant Pot® will start on its own, coming to pressure within a few minutes before counting down the 4 minutes.

When the cooking is done, turn off the Instant Pot®, but do not release the pressure. Set a timer for 4 minutes to let the eggs finish cooking. After the 4 minutes have elapsed, release the last of the pressure from the valve and open the lid.

Place the hard-boiled eggs in a bowl of cold tap water for 5 minutes before peeling them.

Electric Steamer Method

Fill the electric steamer with water according to the manufacturer's directions (usually there is a line indicating the fill level). Place the steamer container on the steamer. Place 3 to 12 eggs inside the steamer container and put the lid on the steamer.

Set the steamer for 15 minutes. After the 15 minutes have elapsed, place the hard-boiled eggs in a bowl of cold tap water for a few minutes before peeling them.

Stovetop Method

Place the eggs in a pot large enough for all 3 to 12 eggs to sit on the bottom of the pot. Fill the pot with water to cover the eggs by 1 inch (2.5 cm).

Heat the pot until the water is just boiling, and then remove the pot from the heat, letting the eggs stand in the hot water for 12 minutes.

Place the hard-boiled eggs in a bowl of cold tap water for a few minutes before peeling them.

Fast and Frugal Instant Pot® Beans

(dairy-free, egg-free, gluten-free, nut-free, soy-free)

The Instant Pot® has been a game changer in my kitchen for ensuring that real sprouted beans are included in my family's meal plan on a more regular basis. Skipping the can means you are able to soak and sprout the beans to eliminate the gassy properties of the beans, leaving you with freezer-safe bags filled with an easy, protein-rich addition to any lunchbox salad, bean dip, soup, and so much more!

Yield varies

1:3 ratio dried beans to water or broth (see Notes)

Notes

- Do not fill your Instant Pot® more than halfway; 2 cups (400 g) of beans to 6 cups (1.4 L) water is the max you'll be able to fit in a 6-quart (5.7-L) Instant Pot®.

- I have noticed that salting the dry beans before cooking does change the cook time—you will need a longer cook time, and it varies so much that I have decided I prefer how consistently the beans cook when I don't salt them.

Soak the beans to eliminate the gassy properties of the beans. Put the beans in a bowl and cover them with water by a few inches. Cover the bowl with a towel, and leave the bowl at room temperature for 8 to 12 hours. Drain and rinse the beans after soaking.

Put the correct amount of water in the Instant Pot® according to the 1:3 ratio. Add the beans, place the lid on the Instant Pot®, and close the valve.

Press the Bean/Chili button and set the timer for the correct time depending on the type of beans you are cooking:

Chickpeas: 10 minutes

Black beans: 8 minutes

Kidney beans: 7 minutes

Navy beans: 5 minutes

Pinto beans: 4 minutes

Set the pressure level to high. The Instant Pot® will take about 10 minutes to come to pressure before the timer starts.

Once the beans are done cooking, turn the Instant Pot® off and let the pressure release naturally for 10 minutes. After 10 minutes, release the rest of the pressure from the valve, take the lid off, and drain the remaining cooking liquid using a strainer.

To freeze the beans, cool them completely and store them flat in freezer-safe bags for up to 6 months. An alternate option for freezing is to portion out what you typically use for a particular recipe and freeze just that much. For instance, for the Colorful Rainbow Pinwheels (page 15), you could portion out 1-cup (165-g) baggies of chickpeas and store those in a large freezer-safe bag so the right amount of beans is easy to grab.

Prep-Day Whole Chicken Two Ways

(dairy-free, egg-free, gluten-free, nut-free, soy-free)

My entire kitchen routine revolves around my weekly chicken. My hope is that once you get into your kitchen flow, you'll see how the simple practice of cooking a nourishing pastured chicken every week will fill your meal gaps week in and week out—it's perfect for busy families!

Makes 6 to 7 cups (840 to 980 g) shredded or cubed chicken (depending on the size of the bird)

2 cups (480 ml) water

1 medium onion, coarsely chopped

2 medium carrots, coarsely chopped

2 medium ribs celery, coarsely chopped

4 cloves garlic, smashed

1 (5- to 6-lb [2.3- to 2.8-kg]) whole pastured chicken

Sea salt and black pepper, as needed (optional)

Dried thyme and parsley, as needed (optional)

Place the water, onion, carrots, celery, and garlic in the bottom of an Instant Pot® or a slow cooker. Place the whole chicken, breast down, on top of the water and veggies. If you want to season your chicken, sprinkle it with the sea salt and black pepper (if using) and the thyme and parsley (if using).

If you are using a slow cooker, place the lid on the slow cooker and cook the chicken on low for 8 to 9 hours.

If you are using an Instant Pot®, place the lid on the Instant Pot® and make sure the valve is closed. Press the Poultry button, and set the timer for 28 minutes. The Instant Pot® will turn on automatically and will take about 10 minutes to come to pressure before counting down the 28 minutes. When the cooking has finished, unplug the Instant Pot® and let the chicken rest for 10 minutes before releasing the remaining pressure.

When the chicken is done cooking, regardless of which cooking method you have used, pull the chicken out to debone it on a cutting board and strain the juices out to use as broth.

Notes

- The juices left over from cooking your chicken are called meat stock. It is a bit different from bone broth but still highly nutritious. You can use meat stock just like broth in any soup recipe.

- I tend to leave my chicken unseasoned so that I can season it how I want for the recipe that I am using it in.

- Be sure to keep the bones to make your own slow cooker or Instant Pot® bone broth in the next recipe! You can store the bones in the fridge for up to 2 days or freeze them for up to 3 months.

Simple Nourishing Bone Broth

(dairy-free, egg-free, gluten-free, nut-free, soy-free)

While bone broth is a buzzword these days, the practice of making nourishing broths from pastured animals has been around for ages, fueling just about every culture. Making your own bone broth will not only save your budget and loads of cooking time, but it will also deeply nourish your family with nutrients that can only come from scratch-made soup.

Makes 16 cups (3.8 L)

Bones from 1 to 3 whole chickens (page 164)

2 medium carrots, coarsely chopped

2 medium ribs celery, coarsely chopped

4 cloves garlic

2 tbsp (30 ml) apple cider vinegar or white wine

Water, as needed

Sea salt, as needed (optional; see Notes)

Black pepper, as needed (optional; see Notes)

Put the bones, carrots, celery, and garlic in a slow cooker or an Instant Pot®. Pour in the vinegar and enough water to cover the bones and veggies. Season the mixture with sea salt (if using) and black pepper (if using). Let this mixture sit at room temperature for 30 minutes to soak.

If you are using a slow cooker, cook the bones and veggies on low for 24 hours. Strain the broth out into jars.

If you are using an Instant Pot®, place the lid on the Instant Pot® and make sure the valve is closed. Press the Manual button, and set the timer for 120 minutes. The pressure cooker will start automatically, taking about 10 minutes to come to pressure before counting down the 120 minutes. After the broth is done cooking, release the pressure and strain the broth out into jars.

To freeze the broth, let the broth cool completely in the refrigerator, then transfer it to the freezer without a lid to freeze for 24 hours before adding a lid. BPA-free freezer-safe containers work well for freezing broth too. Bone broth will keep for 7 days in the refrigerator and for up to 3 months in the freezer.

Notes

- I leave my broth unseasoned for sea salt and pepper so that I can season it according to whatever soup I am making.
- I keep the bones from my weekly roasted chicken in a large freezer-safe bag in the freezer, and when I have saved up the bones from 2 or 3 whole chickens, I make broth. That way, I'm not having to make broth weekly—just once a month or so.

Acknowledgments

I knew from the minute *Nourished Beginnings Baby Food* was published that I wanted to write a sequel. Babies don't stay babies! They grow into little people that still need to be fed well, and I wanted to help moms make that transition from babyhood to school age without compromising the real-food foundations that they set in those first few years. But I also wanted to reach a broader audience of moms. Some parents don't learn about real food until later, and I wanted them to be able to pick up this book, be empowered, feel some grace, and know that they could do this as well. With my oldest entering middle school, and all three girls in full-time school for several years now, the timing was right.

My first book-writing experience was a whirlwind of weekly kitchen tornadoes and marathon library sessions, mixed with the exhausting everyday life of a stay-at-home mom of three, a life filled with sloppy kisses, diapers, tantrums, and school. And yet when I ran the idea of a second book past my husband, it was without hesitation that he said, "It is needed, and you really should do it." We held hands and plunged feet first into writing another book as a family team. My kitchen, a perpetual mess, was lovingly cleaned without question. My frantic calls to my husband when I needed more of an ingredient that I ran out of after attempt five of a recipe were met with a chuckle and a grocery bag full of food. He spent countless nights waiting patiently for me as I finished up at the computer well after dark, so I didn't have to go to bed alone. Christopher, thank you for holding us all together and helping me get this project done without disrupting our family time and the girls. I love you more with every day.

My sweet babies—Chloe, Claire, and Caitlyn—you are at the forefront of my mind with every recipe written and every word typed. You have given me a passion, and I see world changers in each of you. I am so honored to be your momma and to get to watch you grow every day.

There is a huge tribe of friends that have surrounded me during this project. Thank you to my blogging friends and mentors, who always surround me with writing support and wisdom. I do not forget where I've come from, and I have so many of you to thank for that. With age and wisdom, I have also learned the vital necessity of in-person friendships, and my tribe is second to none. To my local tribe of friends—you know who you are—I am the most blessed person in the world to have your friendship. Thank you for all of the last-minute school-pickup help, for the "just because" texts to cheer me on, for making me get out of the house to take a coffee break, and for countless "you can do this" hugs. I am honored to call you my tribe.

To my publisher and editor at Page Street Publishing, Will and Sarah, thank you for believing in this project and for making my dream of a second book a reality.

Thank you to my parents for believing in every passionate idea that comes to me. I didn't need as much physical help with the kids this time around while I wrote since they were in school, but I felt your prayers every day, and I thank God for the faith that you taught me from a very young age.

And finally . . . you, my readers. Thank you for asking me to write another book. I pinch myself every day that I get to turn on my computer, communicate with you, and call this my work. This passion to see the next generation know where their food comes from is becoming a reality because of you. Thank you for running alongside me to ensure that our kids' generation can grow up with real, whole foods and have healthy, sound bodies and minds.

About the Author

Renee Kohley is a wife and momma of three, the author of *Nourished Beginnings Baby Food*, and the vision behind Raising Generation Nourished (raisinggenerationnourished .com). She grew up right in the middle of the low-fat, low-calorie Standard American Diet era, and after she spent years healing her own health issues with whole foods and lifestyle changes, a passion grew in her to see the next generation of kids grow up healthier, love real food, and know where it comes from.

Renee has spent years developing a manageable method for packing school lunches using whole foods to nourish growing bodies, leading to laser-focused kids ready to learn all day at school. Her real-world approach incorporates simple, real food in a kid-friendly way without spending endless time in the kitchen. She lives with her family in Grand Haven, Michigan.

Index